Sicilian Family Adventures

Celia A. Milano

Sicilian Family Adventures
Copyright ©Celia A. Milano 2018
ISBN: 978-1-7320865-7-9
Library of Congress Control Number: 2018913626

Photos by Celia A. Milano unless specified

La Maison Publishing, Inc.

Maison

Vero Beach, Florida
The Hibiscus City
www.lamaisonpublishing.com

"To have seen Italy without seeing Sicily, is not to have seen Italy at all, for Sicily is the clue to everything."
                                                                    Goethe

Foreword

Unofficially, I am the family genealogist and have been researching our history for over twenty years. All the information resides in a software package (Roots Magic) and periodically, I send out an updated version, either paper or electronic, of my family history book, "So Where Do I Really Come From?" to various family members. Recently my oldest nephew, Arthur, called and thanked me for the update of birth, baptism, marriage, immigration, and death information. Then he asked me, "I know you and Mom (my older sister Laurette) took some road trips related to finding information but you never wrote about those. Why not?" I told him that I didn't think anyone in the family would be interested. He convinced me by saying, "We all would like to know." So, here it is...

Table of Contents

Starting the Journey to Discovery

It all started when I received a small package from my mother. When I opened the envelope, there was a note explaining the contents.

It continued an old conversation regarding that timeless question, "Where did we come from?" As a little girl, I always asked my parents where our family came from. I was always told, "We are American, and we are from New York City." But why do Grandma and Grandpa Milano have a funny way of speaking? No answer. Little did I know that those of different ethnicity (German, Italian and Japanese) were discriminated against in the 1920's, 30's, 40's and 50's in New York City and were sent to internment camps. I just discovered this piece of ugly history.

Now I was intrigued. I had a million things going through my mind, but, mostly, what was Mom really looking for when she stumbled upon these items? That aside, I looked at the smaller enclosed envelope, which had a child's drawing of a pelican, my favorite bird. I hoped it was a good omen. As I opened the envelope, I saw a bundle of tissue paper. I gingerly opened it and found very old documents. I was so excited! It was like hitting the jackpot at Harrah's. Maybe not to those who love the excitement of the casinos, but it was for me.

I carefully began to look through the documents. A few of them were so old and scotch-taped together I was afraid to touch them. But what a treasure trove of information my mother had gifted to me. Included were birth, immigration, and death certificates for my grandparents. Now that I had these documents, I couldn't wait to get started. My organizational skills kicked in and I grabbed my computer coding sheets to begin my flowchart. And, of course, this led to many unanswered questions.

I called Mom and started the cross-examination. My mother was a woman of very few words, especially about the family. I asked her, "Grandpa Cottone's death certificate says he was born in Italy. Do you know where?" Mom said, "Papa came from Messina." I said, "Okay, Ma, but Messina is both a city and a province in Sicily."

After that conversation, I did some research and found some tools to help with my next step. The Stato Civile in the Comune of Messina, Sicily, Italy, accepts requests for birth, death, and marriage extracts. http://www.comune.messina.it/.

On the Church of Jesus Christ of the Latter-Day Saints (Mormons) website, I found a form letter for my requests. https://familysearch.org/ I started out with a basic one but then began tweaking it to add the information I had. I used multiple translation websites, including Babelfish, Systran and Alta Vista to help translate my Word document into Italian. Why?

Because this was before Google Translate existed. So, I composed the letter, sent it the Stato Civile in Messina and crossed my fingers.

I also went online, to the Italian White Pages, http://www.paginebianche.it/, searched for folks with the surname of Cottone in Messina and did a "mass mailing" to all of them asking if they were related to my grandfather. Yes, I know...a search for the proverbial needle in a haystack.

PorgendoLe i miei piu sinceri saluti,

Le scrivo questa lettera nella speranza di rintracciare l'albero genealogico della mia famiglia. Il nome del nonno materno di mia madre e Francesco Cottone nato a Messina il 18 agosto 1891 da Antonio Cottone e Tina Truglio Cottone. Alcune storie di famiglia raccontano che egli sia stato l'unico membro della su famiglia a lasciare Messina e venire in America.

Se Lei e imparentato con uno di questi rami sia della famiglia Cottone che Truglio o se ha notizia di mio nonno e della sua famiglia, Le sarei molto grata se Lei potesse aggiornarmi scrivendomi al suddetto indirizzo.

La ringrazio per il suo cortese aiuto et La saluto distintamente.

Two weeks later, I received a reply from the Stato Civile in Messina stating that they had no record of my grandfather, Francesco Cottone.

I called Mom, discussed the letter and she said, "Maybe Margaret could help."

I said, "Okay, but who is Margaret?"

She answered, "Margaret is Carmela's daughter-in-law."

Bewildered I said, "Okay, but who is Carmela?"

Mom replied, "Carmela was Papa's sister."

Stunned I said, "Really? You mentioned this in your note, but I was never told this. Why? Where does she live?"

Mom gave me Margaret's phone number in upstate New York but before I called Margaret, I spoke with my older sister Laurie. She said that she, Mom and Dad would go up to "the farm" to visit Aunt Carmela before I was born. I told Laurie that I was going to call Margaret, introduce myself, and ask if we could visit.

Road trip!

Road Trip

Circa 1950: Laurie (on left), Great-Aunt Carmela (middle) and Cousin
Michael (on right) at "the farm" in Port Jervis NY. Photo by L.V.M.

I called Margaret, introduced myself and spoke about the family and
my research. She said, "Yes, my mother-in-law, Carmela, was the sister
of your grandfather Frank."

I couldn't believe it. All these years.

She was excited to hear from me and we decided on a date to meet. Two weeks later, on a gorgeous Saturday morning, I drove ninety miles to my sister Laurie's house in Oakland, New Jersey. After having coffee and talking, it was time to go. Laurie wanted to drive.

Yikes!

My sister thought she was a great driver...not. It was a bumpy and terrorizing seventy-mile ride to Port Jervis, New York.

Thankfully, we found the house with the covered front porch. Even before we opened the car doors, a tall thin woman was running to the car and greeted us by saying, "Hello, my name is Margaret. Oh my, Laurette, is that you?"

Incredible!

Introductions were made and Margaret showed us around the house and the outdoor garden or "the farm" that my sister mentioned earlier. We chatted and had a light lunch with wine. Margaret told us that there was a trunk in the attic that we needed to see. A short time later, the kitchen door opened and a man and two girls entered. Margaret introduced her son Michael (in the photo) and his two daughters.

Unbelievable! More cousins.

After lunch, Michael brought the trunk down from the attic and opened a box nestled inside it.

Oh my God!

There were many documents inside. The most important – the birth certificate of Camilla (aka Carmela) Cottone. The city of birth listed was Librizzi in the province of Messina. So, we now knew the city where our grandfather was born. After this discovery, we had coffee and then went to the local cemetery to pay our respects to our relatives.

Later that evening on the way home, Laurie asked me, "Now what?" I told her I needed to obtain the address for the Comune in Librizzi, Messina, Sicily, Italy, and write another letter.

Sardinia, Palermo, Cefalu...

In 1995, a year before the road trip with my sister Laurie to Port Jervis in 1996, I had to book our timeshare for 1997. FYI: With the Mediterranean Timeshare Ownership group, we always had to book our weeks two years in advance. Since the timeshare was in Spain, my husband, Vito, and I usually returned to Fuengirola for at least two weeks and enjoyed the time with wonderful friends, Monika, Freddy, Zala, Seb, Gerardo and a cast of other characters.

But in 1997, I wanted to go to Sicily. I had never been there but something was pulling at me to go. Vito wasn't thrilled with the idea as he enjoyed Spain. After much discussion and research, I booked a week on the island of Sardinia and a week in the town of Cefalu in northern Sicily.

Previously, I mentioned that I mailed letters to those living in Messina with the surname of Cottone and hoped I would receive at least one reply. Fast forward, to May 1997. Two days before we left for our Sardinia / Sicily trip, I received a reply to one of my letters. I couldn't believe it! The letter was from a Signora Carolina Puleo.

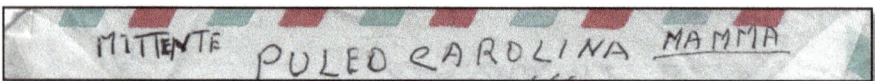

I wanted to reply but decided that I would try to contact the Signora when we were in Sicily. How? I had no clue, but that letter burned a hole in my pocket the whole time we were in Sardinia.

The Emerald Coast of Sardinia was absolutely gorgeous. We stayed at a wonderful timeshare in Cannigione, "Sporting Hotel Tanca Manna," where all the people we met were very welcoming and friendly. I don't know if I mentioned before that Vito's first language was a Neapolitan dialect, thanks to Grandma Adelina Colicchio. So, when he spoke with some of the staff, they immediately called him, "Hey Na-poli-tan."

Sardinia, the Emerald Coast – 1997

After a week of soaking up the sun, time at the beach, finding great restaurants and exploring the island, it was time to fly from Olbia, Sardinia to Palermo, Sicily. Since we had a one-day lag between checking out of the first timeshare and checking into the second one, we booked into the President Hotel overseeing the port of Palermo. How we got there was a miracle. There are NO street signs in Palermo, as they are embedded into the cornerstones of buildings. So, unless you drove on the sidewalks, which the Vespas (small motor scooters) were doing, you had no clue.

As Vito was driving around in the city, with our luggage piled in the car, an angel in the next car asked, "Dove stai andando? (Where are you going?)"

We replied, "Il porto. (The port.)"

She asked, "L'aeroporto? (The airport?)"

We said, "No, la marina. (The marina.)"

She said, "Vieni seguimi. (Follow me.)" That angel led the way right to the front of the hotel.

Grazie Signora!

During the course of the day, Vito, who was in the hotel business, did his networking among the staff. In speaking with the concierge, Giovanni, he mentioned the letter I received right before we left. Giovanni took the information, called the family in Messina and then told us that we were invited for Sunday dinner at their home.

Holy cow!

We couldn't thank him enough. I was stunned.

The next day, we checked out of the hotel and drove east to the timeshare in Cefalu, "Mazzaforno Sporting Club," our home base for the next week.

Flowers by the pool

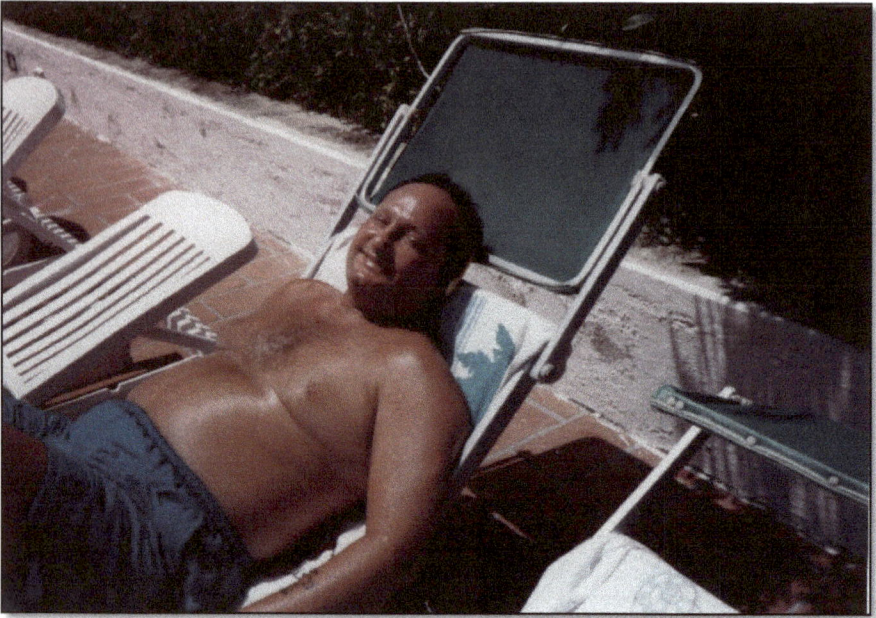

Vito enjoying the sun

We spent the next day exploring in the town of Cefalu, especially the Piazza Duomo where the Norman Cathedral is located. The Normans conquered Sicily in 1091 and the construction on the cathedral began in 1131 and finished over one hundred years later. Both the piazza and the cathedral are overwhelming and the architecture is spectacular.

Norman Cathedral Piazza Duomo - 1997

Street in Cefalu - 1997

Messina

Signora Carolina

Signora Rosa

On Sunday morning, we started our trip to Contesse, a municipality of Messina where the Cottone family was waiting for us. We drove east on the A20 Highway until the road was blocked by a mountain (yes, a mountain with no tunnel). We then had to take the sea road, with only a single lane in either direction, for about 45 kilometers (28 miles). Then back up to the A20 Highway, which you can see from the sea road. Too weird! All in all, it was about a two-hour ride and one hundred ten miles.

Once in Contesse, Vito stopped at an Agip gas station to ask for directions, but the attendant decided to call the house for us. Lo and behold, shortly thereafter, our rescuer arrived and told us to follow him. When we arrived at the house, there was a street party in progress. Folks were barbecuing on the sidewalk and the whole family was there to welcome us. It felt like Christmas.

Vito was able to communicate with everyone and was our translator for the day. Some of the young ladies spoke English, so I was also able to understand what was being said. After getting acquainted, the feasting began.

After dinner, all of us crammed into cars and went to another relative's home on the Straits of Messina. What a fantastic day with a very loving family. Grazie Signora Carolina and Signora Rosa!

We spent the rest of the week exploring the town of Cefalu and the surrounding areas. It was a fantastic two weeks and then back to the States.

Cottone, Puleo, and LoDuca families – 1997

Beach at the Straits of Messina – Sicily side – 1997

Beach house at the Straits of Messina – Sicily side – 1997

A Surprise from Librizzi Messina

Thanks to Cousin Margaret, we now knew that Grandpa Francesco
Cottone was born in Librizzi in the province of Messina. His parents
were Antonio Cottone and Tindala Truglio and he had a sister
Carmela. In November 1998, I wrote to the Ufficio dello Stato Civile
in Librizzi, Messina, Italy, requesting the birth certificate for my
grandfather and any other family documents.

---

12 novembre 1998

Cumune di Librizzi
Librizzi, Messina 98064 Italy

PorgendoLe i miei piu sinceri saluti,

*Vi sarei grato se poteste cercare i seguenti atti e dopo spedirmi gli estratti
coi nami dei genitori:*

- *Il certificato di nascita di mio nonno Francesco Cottone nato a Librizzi,
  Messina il 18 agosto 1891 da Antonio Cottone e Tina (Tindala) Truglio.*
- *Il Certificato di Stato di famiglia di Matrimonio*
- *I certificati di decesso de Antonio Cottone (il padre de Francesco
  Cottone) e Tindala Truglio Cottone (la madre de Francesco Cottone).*
- *I certificati di nascita de Antonio Cottone (il padre de Francesco
  Cottone) e Tindala Truglio Cottone (la madre de Francesco Cottone).*

*Accludo $5. In caso fosse insufficiente, vi prego di informarmi circa
l'ulteriore somma da spedire.*

Vi ringrazio sentitamente per il Vostro aiuto.

Cordialmente,

Simultaneously, I did a mailing to anyone with the Cottone surname in Librizzi. I introduced myself, wrote a little about the known family history, and asked that if they were of this family line, would they be kind enough to contact me.

In December 1998, I received a letter from a Signor Giuseppe Cottone. He wrote that he was astonished and curious that someone from America was inquiring about the Cottone family. He believed that were third or fourth cousins (to be determined). He also stated that while I waited to hear from the Ufficio, he included two birth certificate extracts. One was Francesco's and the other was for Anna Cottone, Francesco's sister.

Another great-aunt!

I was surprised that he, and not the Ufficio, was the first to send the certificates. Although, the town was very small, with less than 2000 people, and I assumed that when the letters arrived for each Cottone family, it must have been a surprise for all of them. I was sure they all conferred with one another and Signor Cottone took the lead.

Shortly thereafter, the Ufficio sent the same birth certificates along with my great-grandparents' birth, marriage and death information.

The Search in Western Sicily

At the same time, I had begun researching my paternal side of the family. Based on the birth certificates Mom gave me, I had written to both the Comune in Trapani and Castellammare del Golfo. No replies. Maybe my requests were not communicated properly, but I was not deterred.

I went online, again, to the Italian white pages, and began entering all the surnames for Dad's side of the family – Milano, Galatioto, Vivona, and Sceusa. There were many names listed for Castellammare del Golfo, so I began comparing the names and addresses. As there were some duplicates, I eliminated them from the list.

I then began composing my letter: introduction, explanation of my research, list of great-grandparents, their children, how I was related, knowledge of the family and closing. I then translated the letter from English to Italian using Babelfish and Altavista. As I stated before, Google translate did not exist yet. Unfortunately, the Sicilian dialect was not available through either Babelfish or Altavista, so Italian was my only choice.

I printed out fifty-four letters, trekked to the post office where the postal clerks knew me by name and had the international stamps ready for me. I mailed them and now it was time to wait...again.

On Valentine's Day 1998, I received an airmail envelope with Dad's name, Lorenzo Milano, on the return address. I froze, as on this day fifteen years earlier, we buried Dad.

Way too coincidental!

As I opened the envelope, I saw that the letter was typed and written in dialect. I tried to translate it as best I could but I knew I needed help. So, I called The Language School, in Red Bank, New Jersey, as everyone there knew of my research. The fact that I was there with an "incoming" letter in hand was unreal. They had all warned me that answers might not be forthcoming, as outsiders were not easily let in.

But one gentleman had replied. He said that he and many other family members, with the same and different surnames, received letters. They all went to him, Lorenzo, to see if I was legitimate. He vouched for me as I had included information not included in official records. It turned out that he was Dad's first cousin.

Unbelievable!

Thus, began the correspondence between us and many visits to The Language School. But as time rolled on, I decided it was time to meet this wonderful man.

I told my sister Laurie (Laurette) that we were going to Sicily. She thought I meant Vito and myself, but I told her that, no, she was going. She panicked. Laurie had never been out of the country and didn't have a passport, so that was the first thing she needed. She hyperventilated throughout the entire paperwork process.

In April 1999, I wrote to Lorenzo to tell him that my sister and I were planning a trip to meet him and his family. Really, I was planning it, as my sister had no clue as to what needed to be done.

I had checked with the timeshare company and there weren't any properties in the area. I wrote to Lorenzo and asked him to recommend a nearby hotel or bed and breakfast. He wrote back and said that he and his wife Maria would be hosting us, meaning that we would be staying with them. I was totally stunned. Strangers, whom he'd never met. He said he would be honored to host his Uncle Rosario's granddaughters.

Arrangements were made. I told Lorenzo that we would be in Rome for four days, then fly to Palermo, drive to my timeshare in Falcone for a week to visit Signor Cottone in Librizzi and see the town, and then drive to Castellammare del Golfo.

A Funny Thing Happened at the Hotel Quirinale

Everything was set. My sister and I left from the Newark New Jersey Airport and arrived in Rome-Fiumicino Airport the next morning. I made prior arrangements for a car service to take us from the airport to the hotel, as I didn't want the hassle of flagging down a taxi. The driver gave us a tour of Rome along the way to the Hotel Quirinale, our home for four days.

We reached the hotel and checked in. I told my sister to select her bed, get freshened up and then we had things to do. She balked, as her head was still spinning from jetlag and all the sights and sounds coming from the Rome airport. She was also eyeing the bed and giving me the evil eye at the same time.

We needed two things: First, strong coffee and then I needed to speak with the concierge about how to obtain tickets for St. Peter's Basilica, the Vatican Museum and Sistine Chapel tours. These were our "must see" places. The young concierge agreed and gave us directions to the ticket vendor.

Views from our room at the Hotel Quirinale in Rome – 1999

Okay, after the concierge, we were out the door and on our way to the Espresso Bar. You've got to love the Romans – cars and scooters were lined up and running while their drivers and passengers ran inside to gulp down a shot or two of caffé normale (what we know as espresso). It was my kind of place.

We found the ticket office and purchased tickets for the next morning's Vatican tour. Laurie finally understood that, as a tourist, you cannot procrastinate while in Rome. You need to have your plans set and pace yourself. We walked around the city to get our bearings and arrived at the Colosseum, which was incredible. The amphitheatre was built between 72AD and 80AD and could seat approximately 70,000 spectators for the gladiator competitions, executions and animal hunts. We ventured to various areas of the arena imagining all that had occurred there.

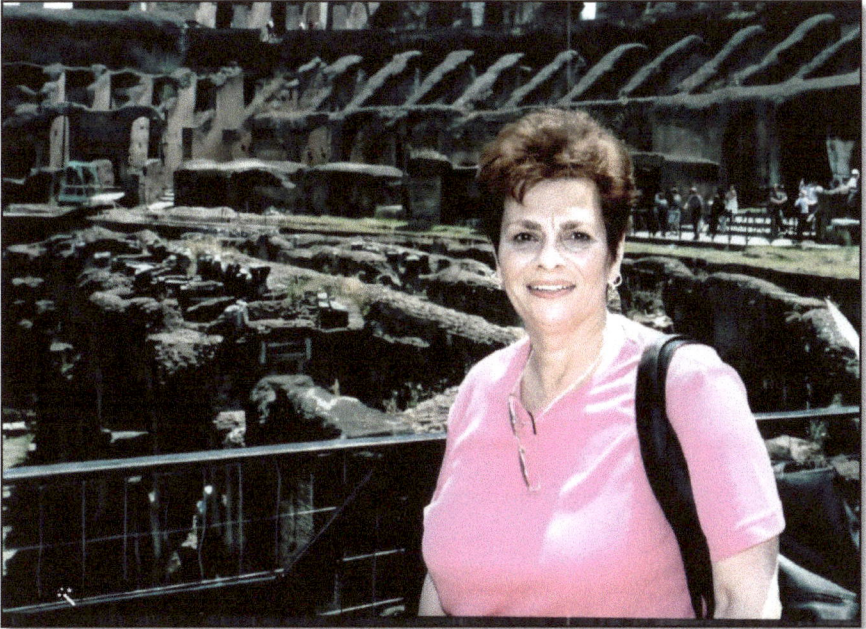

Laurie in the Colosseum in Rome – 1999

After our morning excursion, we headed back to the hotel to rest. As soon as we entered our room, the phone rang. We just looked at each other, as only three people knew we were in Rome – Vito, my niece Lori and our cousin Lorenzo in Castellammare del Golfo. I answered the phone and a lady spoke to me in what I call machine-gun Italian.

I said, "Signora, no parlo Italiano."

She hung up. A few minutes later the phone rang again. This time it was a gentleman named Alfonso, who spoke English, and explained that the Signora Maria, who called, was the sister of Lorenzo in Sicily. She wanted to meet us, so arrangements were made.

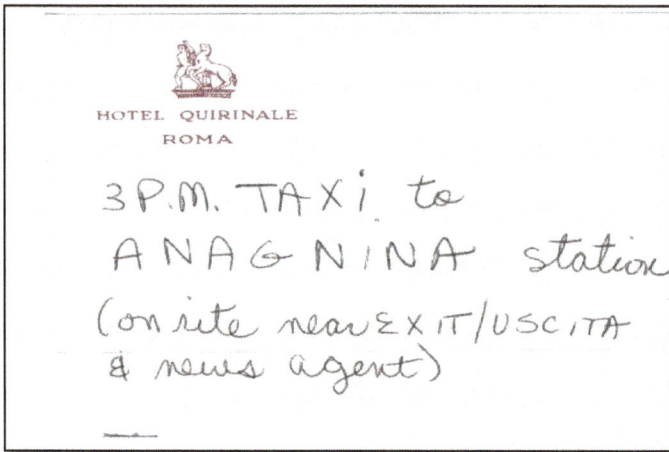

HOTEL QUIRINALE
ROMA

3 P.M. TAXi to
ANAGNINA station
(on rite near EXiT/USCiTA
& news agent)

During the call, I could see that Laurie was freaking out, as she thought her daughter Lori, who was going through chemotherapy, was calling. When the call ended, Laurie just looked at me and asked what just happened. I told her that we will be meeting Lorenzo's sister, Signora Maria and her family the day after tomorrow. Little did we know what other surprises awaited us.

The next day Laurie and I took the tours of St. Peter's Basilica, Vatican Museum and Sistine Chapel. We also went to the Trevi Fountain and the Roman Forum. All the places we wanted to see and more. Plus, we went to every espresso bar and many cafes to sample all the delicious food. We soaked up all the sights and sounds of Rome.

Trevi Fountain and St. Peter's Square 2000 celebration – 1999

Time to Meet Cousins in Rome

The next day, we were excited and nervous at the same time. As we were getting ready to take a cab to the train station to meet Alfonso, the young hotel concierge told us that there was yet another train strike but "no problem getting a taxi."

We arrived at the designated station and, shortly thereafter, we were approached by a gentleman identifying himself as Alfonso, son-in-law of Cousin Maria and accidental interpreter for the day. We learned that Alfonso was a professor who taught English at the university. Introductions were made – Cousin Maria, her husband, Giuseppe, their daughter Vera and her husband, Alfonso. We spent the day in a whirlwind, which included driving to the town of Castel Gandolfo, the Pope's summer home, for sightseeing. The town overlooked Lake Albano, a small volcanic crater lake. We had lunch at a local vineyard. It was a wonderful time.

That evening, we spent time at the home of Giuseppe and Maria for coffee and dolce (sweets). Maria was very excited to show us her photo album. As we were viewing the photos, Maria was narrating with Alfonso translating. When Maria turned the page, Laurie and I both gasped. We saw a very familiar Polaroid photo – Laurie's graduation from grammar school with me standing in front of her at the house in Yonkers. I remember seeing the photo at my parents' house.

Laurie's grammar school graduation
June 1958. Photo by L.V.M.

So now, we were curious as to how our photo made its way to Rome. Maria told us that SaSa, Grandma Milano, always sent photos of the family to them. I remember that Grandma always had Daddy take extra photos, but we thought maybe it was "just in case they didn't develop correctly." But the Polaroid photos were the best because you could watch them develop right in front of you. So, if you screwed up the photo, you just took another one. Now we knew better. Grandma was sending them to the family in Italy.

Who knew?

No problem, but there was another reason for all the photos. For all of my life Laurie had been telling me that she had a godchild in Sicily.

Yeah, right.

I could never figure it out, since she never traveled there. Over the years, when I inquired she told me that Grandma Milano said that if little Mariuccia came to visit us in New York, Laurie would be her hostess/sponsor "la madrina." Grandma was sending photos to Maria so she would know about Laurie's life.

Fifty years later, Laurie had finally met little Mariuccia. She couldn't believe it. She was ecstatic. Floored! Stunned! It was unreal. I was very happy as now the mystery of "little Mariuccia" had been solved. A great way to end a very beautiful day.

Cousin Vera, Celia, Cousin Maria, Laurie, and Pino Rome – 1999

Goodbye Rome. Hello Sicily!

After a whirlwind time in Rome, we were off to the airport again, as Laurie and I were flying from Rome to Punta-Raisi Airport in Palermo to begin our second week of adventures. After arriving in Palermo, we picked up the rental car and began our drive east.

Palermo is NOT my favorite city for driving. And yes, I do know how to drive as I learned to drive in New York City. It was still the same as in prior years - the traffic lights meant nothing, the Vespas were still driving on the sidewalks, passing and then shooting out in front of you. It would give anyone agita (heartburn).

I was very relieved to see the eastbound entrance of the A19 Highway, which turned into the A20. We were headed to Falcone in the province of Messina, where I booked a week of timeshare.

It was a two-and-a-half-hour ride and two hundred thirty-three kilometers (145 miles). We soaked up the scenery until we hit a snag.

Laurie freaked out when the autostrada ended at a mountain, and we had to continue down to the sea road for forty-five kilometers then back up to the autostrada, like mountain goats. A hole wasn't blasted through the mountain so the road literally stopped. I told her that Vito and I had the same experience in 1997.

Once we got to Falcone and settled into the timeshare, we took off for a drive around to get our bearings. Along the way we got caught up in a traffic jam...of goats.

Traffic Jam in Falcone – 1999

Then it was back to the timeshare where we met some very nice folks from the U.K. For the next day, all of us booked a ferry trip from the port of Milazzo to Vulcano, one of the Aeolian Islands in the

Tyrrhennian Sea. The concierge mentioned that we should wear old clothes if we wanted to experience the sulfur mud baths. We all looked at each other and shrugged.

Port of Milazzo – 1999

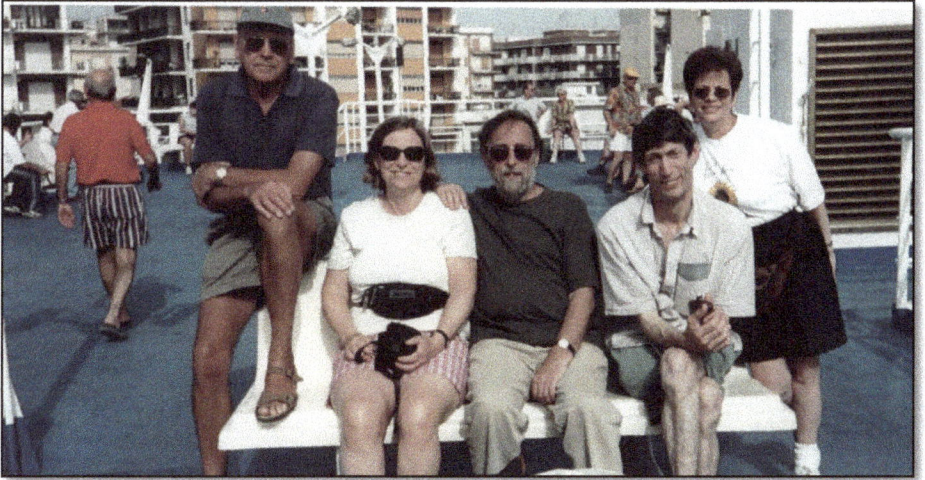

Laurie (far right) with Brits on Ferry – 1999

The ferry ride was great as was the company and sea air. The island of Vulcano is well known for the Fossa di Vulcano, the Great Crater, a smoking volcanic crater and for black sand beaches. We followed the signs to the sulfur baths, which really weren't needed, as the smell of the fumes, like rotting eggs, was unmistakable. Many people were already soaking up the baths. We all ventured in and, wow, the heat was intense. After a while, we understood why we needed to wear old clothes. As the embers from the volcanic activity near the baths came in contact with your clothes, holes were burned into the fabric. Other than that, we really enjoyed ourselves traipsing through the mud. Laurie suggested we cool off in the sea, so she and I headed to Spiaggia di Sabbia Nera, the Black Sand Beach. It was refreshing and we just made it back in time to catch the ferry. We had a great first day and met some wonderful people.

Vulcano Sulfur Baths – 1999

The next day the tour desk concierge suggested we might enjoy going to Tindari, a Greek settlement founded in the fourth century B.C. We did, and saw archaeological excavations, including the mosaic floors that you can see in the photo I took.

Archaeological dig in Tindari - 1999

We also went to the Church of the Black Madonna, high on a hill. The statue of the Black Madonna is said to have come from Constantinople. I tried taking a photo of the Madonna but the gold around it blurred the photo.

Another fantastic day of exploring eastern Sicily!

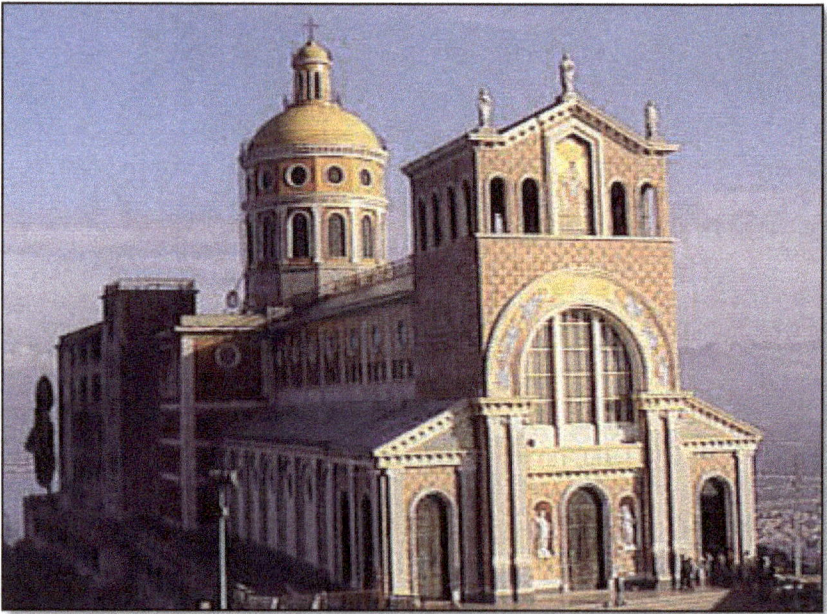

Church of the Black Madonna – 1999

Librizzi

The day had finally come for us to drive to our maternal grandfather's mountain town of Librizzi, north of Patti. It was a very small town of about 2000 people and we were going to meet Signor Cottone, the gentleman I mentioned previously, who responded to my letter.

Librizzi was about twelve miles from Falcone, with half of those climbing the mountain to the town. As we were driving, Laurie and I wondered how Grandpa Cottone ever got down the mountain in 1910 to board a ship from Naples. Did he walk or use a cart and donkey? We'll never know. Laurie was funny, as she started singing, "She'll be coming around the mountain, when she comes."

Librizzi, Messina – 1999

We arrived early as I wanted to go to the Comune (town hall) to thank Roberto, the clerk, for sending me documents. Plus, we just wanted to walk around the town and soak up the atmosphere.

As we strolled, Laurie noticed that people kept glancing at us. It was as if we had a sign on our foreheads saying "Tourist." We weren't aware at the time, but since the town was small and everyone knew everyone, we stuck out like two sore thumbs. After walking around, we sat in the shade to rest. Now that I look back on it, we may have taken someone's regular spot.

Piazza in Librizzi – 1999

At this point, a gentleman approached us and asked, "Tu chi sei? (Who are you?)" I told him we were of the Cottone family and meeting Giuseppe Cottone. I had the postal envelope with me, which I showed him. He then motioned for us to follow him, and he brought us directly to the address. Laurie thanked him, we knocked on the door and were warmly greeted by Signor Giuseppe and his lovely wife Signora Elisa.

We spent a wonderful day with Giuseppe (Pino), Elisa and their daughter Annalisa. Of course, language was a problem but Giuseppe solved that with a translation CD on his computer. (Remember folks, this was in 1999 before all the internet translation options). I thanked him for responding to my original correspondence and sending additional documents from the town hall. Annalisa was very kind and took us on a walking tour including the cemetery.

To this day, we have not established a direct family connection but keep in touch, via Facebook, with Pino (Giuseppe), Annalisa and Tamara, their oldest daughter.

Piazza Catena in Librizzi

Castellammare del Golfo and Beyond

We had a great time sightseeing and meeting new people but the week flew by and it was time to hit the road, as we had a very special meeting scheduled later in the day. I drove and Laurie was in charge of the maps, kilometers and toll info. It is approximately a three-hour drive and 240 kilometers (150 miles).

On our drive west, we stopped in Cefalu, as I wanted to show my sister the town, especially the Norman Cathedral, which she loved seeing. We also strolled around the piazza and went to my favorite jewelry store, owned by Signor Delas, to buy matching bracelets.

1997

Afterwards, we continued our journey to Castellammare del Golfo in western Sicily, which included driving through parts of Palermo, which, as you know from my previous adventures, is not a driver-friendly city. As I drove, Laurie kept up a continuing monologue of the sights and drivers.

Finally, I saw the exit and couldn't believe we were already there. We stopped at the Belvedere to take a photo of our second ancestral village, Castellammare del Golfo.

Castellammare del Golfo, Trapani, Sicily – 1999

We continued on to the designated bar, had some caffé normale and waited for our cousin Lorenzo Milano. From where we were sitting, folks coming through the door looked like shadows. But the minute Lorenzo walked in, I saw the outline of Dad – the shape of the head, the shoulders, hips and height. It was surreal. After hugs, kisses and more caffé normale, we were off. Lorenzo and his wife Maria were hosting us at their beautiful house in town. We had no idea that it meant Maria and Lorenzo literally gave us their townhouse to stay in while they stayed at their cottage in the vineyard.

47

View From The Townhouse – 1999

Laurie and I were astonished by their kindness. The townhouse was absolutely beautiful and all the balconies, plus the rooftop, had views of the gulf. Absolutely spectacular.

We didn't realize it at the time, but once we'd settled in, we were off on another whirlwind tour. We were thrilled.

The next morning, as we finished dressing, the doorbell rang. I went down two levels to answer the door. It was Cousin Lorenzo, smiling.

He said, "Permisso?"

He was asking permission to come into the house, his own house. Oh my God! Such a gentleman.

Lorenzo was so excited that morning. He said, "Andiamo! (Let's go!)"

He took us on a walking tour of the town showing us where all the family had once lived, including my grandfather, Rosario Milano, who was Lorenzo's uncle. Along the way, he stopped to introduce us to his friends and neighbors, and of course, we stopped to have many caffé normales and stuffed cornettos (croissants).

Afterwards, Lorenzo had me follow him to the vineyard in our rental car. When I first stepped foot on the property, I had a feeling I'd never had before – and I started crying. I felt as if I'd finally arrived home. Lorenzo asked me if I was okay.

I said, "Io sono contento cugino. (I am content cousin.)"

We would spend our afternoons having dinner there, relaxing and walking amongst the vines.

I remember the first afternoon Lorenzo wanted to show us the property, as there were rows of vines all around the cottage and across the road. While Lorenzo was checking the plants, I kept finding small snails in the dirt. I had checked with my dictionary, found the Italian word for snail, lumaca, and tried to pronounce it.

Lorenzo said, "No, babalucie," which is Sicilian dialect for snail. We laughed as he pointed to my very large Cassell's Italian-English Dictionary and said "Il libro. (The book.)"

I consulted it often. It weighed five pounds but I carried it in my backpack everywhere.

The Cottage and Vineyard – 1999

Lorenzo had many excursions planned for us. One day we piled into my rental car and Lorenzo drove us around the small mountain towns for the view, to sample local delicacies and drink the spring water from local fountains. Maria brought some empty jugs with her, and we filled them at each town. The taste of water from the underground springs was indescribably delicious. Another day, we went to the sea towns of San Vito Lo Capo and Scopello.

We also walked in the Zingaro Reserve. Laurie and I were speechless at all the beauty of these towns and wondered why our grandparents had left.

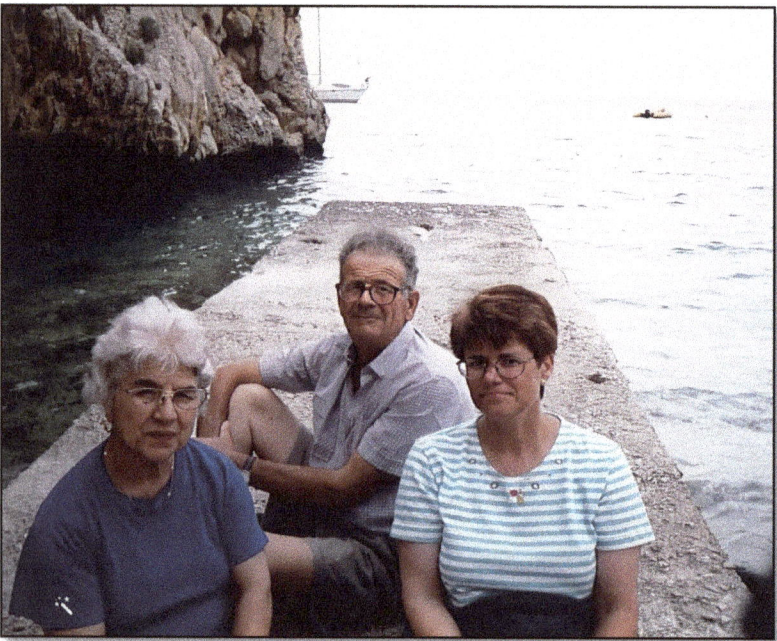

Maria, Lorenzo and Celia in Scopello – 1999. Photo by L.M.Preis

Most importantly, we went to the Comunale Cimiterio, the cemetery, to pay respects to our ancestors. Laurie and I purchased flowers from the vendors outside the gate. As Lorenzo showed us the graves of our relatives, including our great-grandfather Lorenzo, we placed flowers at each grave. Many graves were above ground in mausoleum walls, individual graves, and above ground crypts that house families. Also, most had photographs of the departed on each grave. Now I know why Dad had a photo of his mother, Rosaria Vivona Milano, placed on her gravestone at St. Raymond's Cemetery in the Bronx.

∞∞∞∞

One afternoon, Lorenzo surprised us at his vineyard. He invited some of the relatives that I had written to in my original "mass mailing." Remember, they all went to him when they received the letters asking who I was. After I met them, I had faces to go along with their names. That was also the day we met Lorenzo's older son, Renzo. We were sitting together and everyone would look at him, then at me, and then back at him. They could not get over how similar we looked.

Renzo, our third cousin, spoke English, which his father did not know. Most days, when we had dinner at the vineyard, Lorenzo and Renzo would talk about what we did that day. Renzo was shocked to hear that I had his dad driving the rental car. I said it was easier than opening il libro while driving to search for the words needed to ask for directions. He laughed.

Renzo told me that his father was upset because, when we were leaving after dinner the previous night to return to town, I did not make a full stop at the stop sign. I said that there was a bull in the road, so I thought it best not to stop, and then I motioned with my index fingers up in the air on either side of my head. They both laughed. His father said it was like a pet, very gentle.

Really?

For several days, I was reminded as "the pet" was always standing in the road, but I forced myself to stop at the sign.

∞∞∞∞

Before dinner one evening, Renzo drove Laurie and I to Segesta, to see the ancient Greek temple and amphitheater. Both are in the countryside and, as we approached the temple, the architecture and size were spectacular. It was so unreal to be there.

Celia and Renzo in the Temple at Segesta – 1999. Photo by L.M.Preis

Laurie and Renzo at the amphitheater at Segesta – 1999

Also, Lorenzo planned for us to meet another cousin who lived in Trapani, Lorenzo Milano, also known as "Lorenzene." You must be wondering, "What the heck is it with all these Lorenzos? Why so many in one family?" It's the Italian naming convention as the first-born child is named after the grandfather, in this case Lorenzo. As my dad was named Lorenzo, my sister, being the first-born, was named Laurette, which is an Americanized female form of Lorenzo. (In order

55

to keep track of who's who, I've chosen to use nicknames, hence "Lorenzene.") Lorenzene picked us up at the townhouse and drove west to Marsala, where we had caffé normale at the marina, and then went on to the old town of Gibellina, which was destroyed in the 1968 Belice earthquake.

People lived in makeshift homes until, ten years later, when the new town, Gibellina Nuova, was completed nearby and folks could move in. In 1983 after seeing the old town, the Italian painter and sculptor Alberto Burri decided to make a work of art as a tribute to those who died during the earthquake. As Lorenzene showed us the town from the road, it was very eerie as the whole town had been cemented over by Burri.

Ruderi di Gibellina. Land Art by Alberto Burri.
[http://bit.ly/2Ae3SGR]

At Lorezene's home, we met his wife Francesca, who had prepared a wonderful lunch of salad, pasta, and lamb chops. Scrumptious!

After lunch, we went to the town of Erice to walk and enjoy the afternoon. Erice is a mountain town with cobblestone streets and two churches. At an elevation of approximately 2600 feet, Erice overlooks the town of Trapani and the Tyrhennian Sea.

Francesca insisted that we stop at the famous "Pasticceria Maria Grammatico" for sweets. Okay, so you're now wondering, "Why was it famous?" Maria Grammatico was eleven years old when her mother placed her in the convent, as she could no longer care for her. Maria led a very austere life but learned how to make marzipan, which was how the nuns in all the nearby convents made a living. They were very creative in their designs of the sweets. Maria left the convent after fifteen years and set up her own bakery. The nuns were not happy, and she was banned from ever returning. All of us ordered a different sweet and then shared them. Plus, we bought a tray for Maria and Lorenzo.

Delizioso!

∞∞∞∞

On our last afternoon in Castellammare del Golfo, Laurie, Lorenzo and I walked through the vineyard. I felt overwhelmed but still had a few things on my mind regarding our grandfather, Rosario. Before leaving New Jersey, I painstakingly wrote some information and questions in Italian. I told Lorenzo that I had not been able to find a manifest in the Ellis Island records of Rosario arriving in America. My sister and I could see Lorenzo weighing the pros and cons of answering me. He told me, essentially, that Rosario was only seventeen years old, when he made a jackass out of himself, ticked off "the boss" and had to leave town immediately.

Now what the hell was this all about?

I just stared at Lorenzo and thanked him. I knew when I returned home I would have to research this further.

That night at the townhouse, Laurie said to me "Maybe that explains those little squares of paper."

I said, "What the hell are you talking about?"

She said, "Grandpa always said he worked in the button factory but his hands were never rough. Don't you remember when we went to the candy store near their apartment in the Bronx, he and some of the men exchanged those little white pieces of paper?"

I said, "I was six years old. How would I know?"

Note: Based on records obtained from the US Dept. of Justice, Immigration and Naturalization Service: It was documented that Rosario Milano: "...stated he could not obtain his father's permission to come to the U.S. and as he was under age he had to have that consent, so he came on the passport of a friend of his. He is identified by the scar on his cheek." He sailed under the name of Giovanni Turano on the ship San Giovanni out of the port of Palermo. His Passenger ID 100757160389 Frame 740 and 741 line 29.

∞∞∞∞

Laurie and I could not believe that our time in Sicily was fast coming to an end. The morning we left, Maria and Lorenzo rang the bell asking permission to enter "their" home. Maria was so sweet as she brought caffè normale and sweets for all of us to share before we left.

Maria, Lorenzo, Renzo, and all the relatives are such warm and loving people; they opened their homes, arms, and hearts to family they'd never met. And that relationship did not stop when we returned to the States.

Cousin Lorenzo Milano

Follow-up to the 1999 Italy Adventure

After leaving Italy, Cousin Vera (in Rome) and I continued communicating via email. One email was very interesting as Vera wrote that another cousin, Bernardo, her mother Maria's nephew who lived in Germany, heard about our surprise visit to Rome and was requesting contact information. Vera asked if she could give him my telephone number, as he does not have a computer.

I said, "Of course. But my only misgiving is that I do not speak any Italian nor German."

Vera told me that he spoke the Sicilian dialect, English and German. Bernardo called me and thus began a continuing conversation over the years about the family.

About that time, I was beginning to scan the old photos that my Mom had stashed away in the back of her closet. I told Bernardo many photos were more than likely from Sicily, although they had no writing on the back. Of course, Grandma Milano knew who all those folks were, so there was no need to identify everyone. I recognized Cousin Lorenzo and his wife Maria in one photo, but that was it.

So, Bernardo told me to send him copies and he would obtain the information. A couple of months later, I received my self-addressed envelope back with the information for each person in the photos: name, birth, marriage and/or death information. Another treasure trove of family history.

Cousin Lorenzo in the back with his wife Maria in front of him.

After Many Years ...

After my sister, Laurie, and I went to Rome and Sicily in 1999, and met our wonderful cousins, many things changed. My youngest niece, Lori, Laurie's daughter, lost her battle with cancer at age thirty-four. My "road trip" older sister Laurie died the following year. Mom died three years later and my younger sister, Sarah, died two years after Mom.

For many years, I was deluged with paperwork and lawyers to settle all their life affairs. After my niece died without a will, I begged both my sisters to get wills, living wills, powers of attorney for medical and finance. My sister Laurie saw the struggles I had with her daughter's affairs and did get the four documents, as did Mom, but Sarah didn't.

So, when Sarah died, I had to find a New York attorney and thankfully Cousin Pattie Murano Delgrosso recommended Jim Morris, an absolute treasure. The family tree had to be submitted to the court, including death certificates, which I had. The remaining family also had to agree and notify the court in writing that I be given permission to handle her affairs. Only then were the "Letters of Administration" granted by the court. The most distressing part was dealing with Sarah's boyfriend, who I nicknamed "The Moron." Need I say more?

Ask anyone who knows me and they will tell you that I am always asking people if they have these four documents – will, living will, power of attorney for medical and power of attorney for finances. I know, it does get embarrassing for Vito, but it will save their family a lot of heartache and cursing. Big time cursing.

I had planned two trips to Sicily during those years but had to cancel after Mom died and again after Sarah died. Also, two years after Sarah died in October 2010, I received a fax from Cousin Bernardo informing me that Cousin Lorenzo died. I was devastated. I never saw Lorenzo again, which was my biggest regret.

To keep busy, I joined the local Genealogy Society, co-chaired the Italian Genealogy Interest Group (GIG), with Carol Donofrio Jorgensen, continued researching our family history, and served on the board of directors for The Sicilian Project. But as any genealogist will tell you, there were still many more missing pieces to our family history. As a matter of fact, it is a never-ending story and Sicily had again been calling my name. In response, I answered.

I told Vito I wanted to go back to do more research. He just rolled his eyes. I sent flowers to Cousin Maria with a note saying that I would see her in May. Then I called Cousin Bernardo in Germany to tell him I was going to Castellammare del Golfo, booked a room at Bed and Breakfast Nonna Giò, which Bernardo recommended as it was owned by Cousin-In-Law Felice, and then booked my ticket on Alitalia.

Finally! Back to Sicily

The day had arrived and, of course, it was pouring rain that morning. Vito was upset because he had to drive me to Miami. My flight to Rome was scheduled for 8:35 p.m., but I wanted to be at the airport much earlier, as I'd heard that the TSA lines were very long. Due to the inclement weather, I insisted that Vito stay the night in a hotel rather than drive three hours back home.

Driving south on I-95, the rain let up after an hour and the traffic wasn't too bad. But of course, after we exited for the airport, the traffic at 12:30 p.m. was bumper to bumper and it started pouring again.

People in Florida do NOT know how to drive in the rain.

Unreal!

We found the hotel and checked in. At 5:00 p.m., both Vito and I signed up for the hotel's airport shuttle, as he wanted to make sure I was okay and got to the Alitalia terminal. I had already checked-in online but still had to check my luggage. Alitalia had a section for "Online Check-in Baggage Drop-off," so within fifteen minutes it was done. After many hugs, kisses and warnings, I breezed through TSA and was on my way to Concourse H. The plane, an Airbus A330 with forty plus rows of eight seats, was waiting at the gate.

Lots of people were traveling to Rome, including three small babies. I cringed and, yes, I cursed when I saw them, as I knew it would be a very bad night for me. It was storming again as we were boarding. As soon as everyone was settled, the captain announced that there would be a thirty-minute delay and then made another announcement of another thirty-minute delay. I knew it wasn't going to be good, as I had a two-and-a-half-hour layover in Rome before my flight to Palermo. Finally, after an hour and a half we were eighteenth in line for takeoff.

The crew was great, as were my veggie meals and the onboard digital entertainment. I read, wrote, listened to music and watched a movie, The Intern, which was very funny. Plus, I had an aisle seat, so no climbing over people. BUT, those three babies cried all night like a relay race – one, then the next and then the next. I was right as I did not get one minute of sleep.

Twelve hours of non-stop crying!

It was 1:30 p.m. by the time we landed in Rome, and I was exhausted. Because of the delay out of Miami, I had forty-five minutes to schlep from the international terminal to the domestic terminal, which was, of course, at the other end of the airport. But first I had to go through a TSA check, again, plus go through customs. The customs line moved like a snail and I was worried if I would make my flight to Palermo. Finally, it was my turn and I got through in less than a minute and then flew through the domestic terminal. Unbeknownst to me, the gate number had changed – twice. Alitalia Gate B was the furthest gate in the terminal. I arrived at the gate soaking-wet from running and got in line to board. I made it by the skin of my teeth.

Thank goodness for two cups of caffé normale and a cornetto on the plane. I arrived in Palermo an hour later, went through another baggage check for international travelers, and then exited. I saw the sign with my name and was greeted by my Cousin-In-Law Felice. We had never met but we had corresponded through emails. We had a lot to speak about on the forty-five-minute drive to Castellammare del Golfo.

We arrived at Felice's Bed and Breakfast Nonna Giò. It was adorable. He explained to me that the house belonged to his favorite grandmother, Giovanna, who died in 1997. He added, "The love for this country and the desire to let people know the various beauties of my land gave me the need to give hospitality to my guests, creating rooms with all comforts. In addition, my business is developed in the field of tourist services: transfer to and from airports and excursions for the whole of Sicily." www.nonnagiotransfer.com

Bed and Breakfast Nonna Giò plus Storefront.

Part of the first floor was occupied by his boutique store, Bazar di Nonna Gio. Felice showed me two rooms, one on the second floor, and one on the third floor. I took the room on the second floor. It was very cozy and I would have only one flight of stairs to deal with, which my not-so-young body would appreciate. You need to understand that in most facilities in Italy, the first floor was usually the foyer and the second floor was considered the first floor. Yes, it could be a little confusing, but most bedrooms are on the higher floors.

Felice knew I was exhausted and left me to settle in. But before I closed the door, Cousin Bernardo was climbing the stairs. It was great to finally meet him after years spent talking on the phone. He could see that I was ready to fall down from being tired and told me to rest, as tomorrow he had many plans for me. I slept for twelve solid hours.

My First Day

On my first morning in Castellammare del Golfo, Cousin Felice and I took a walk to the Corso Garibaldi. He introduced me to Vito Alfano, the owner of Gelateria Garibaldi, where I would be having breakfast each morning. I nicknamed it "Café Garibaldi." Yes, I was staying at a B&B but the breakfast was off-site. I enjoyed it, as I was able to people-watch every morning.

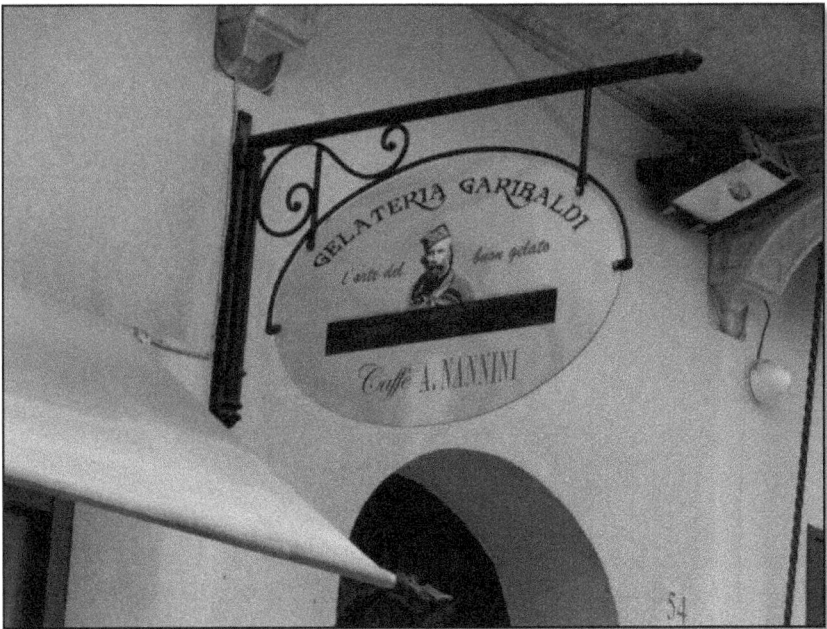

a.k.a. Café Garibaldi – 2016

I headed back to the B&B after breakfast as Felice and his wife, my cousin, Elena, drove us to the car rental agency in town so I could rent a car. During the paperwork process, I added Cousin Bernardo to the drivers' list. "He will be surprised," said Felice. "Yes," I said, "but I am not familiar with the streets so it is best."

Bernardo was waiting when Felice and I arrived back at the B&B. Yes, he was shocked that I added him to the rental policy but said it would be easier getting around than walking. As a matter of fact, we piled into the car immediately. Why? Bernardo knew I was researching several family trees (Milano, Vivona, Giliberti, Sceusa, LaTorre) and had tracked down a gentleman, Vincenzo Vivona. He said, "Andiamo. We are meeting him at another café on the other side of town."

Along the drive, we saw many motorcycles and Bernardo lowered the car window to find out what was happening. He was told that there was going to be a blessing of the helmets at the church.

We continued on to the café and found Signor Vivona, a very charming gentleman. We made introductions, caffé normale ordered and we showed Vincenzo my family tree and book. Vincenzo could not believe that I had so much information. He apologized as he is from another branch of the Vivona family, but he gave me his sister's name and address in Brooklyn, saying, "she may know more information."

Signor Vincenzo Vivona – 2016

Afterwards, we drove out to the countryside to Cousin Lorenzo's vineyard. I got out of the car, walked up the driveway, thought of all the adventures I had had with my sister Laurie and Lorenzo, who were both gone. I took a deep breath. The air was very different from that by the sea. Thinking back, I remembered row after row of vines, there and across the road, walking with Lorenzo and finding small snails in the dirt. Lorenzo laughed when I tried to pronounce the word lumaca, meaning snail. Happy times.

After a while, Bernardo said, "Andiamo, Cousin Maria is waiting for us at my house." Very reluctantly, we left the vineyard. It was wonderful to see Maria again and to be introduced to Vincenza, Bernardo's wife. After more caffè normale, we left with Maria and drove to the Cala Marina in town, which was so packed with cars that you couldn't get through. Yes, it was unreal but that was how it was when Sicilians walk on Sunday. It was called "La Passeggiata Domenica." So, we parked the car on the side of the road and walked. We passed many of the small fishing boats on the left and restaurants on the right. We continued down past The Castle, Al Madarig, which was built by the Arabs and enhanced by the Normans. Bernardo saw many of his friends and introduced me as "Cugina Celia a la America e no parle italiano. (My cousin Celia from America who does not speak Italian.)" I would hear this introduction during my whole stay.

Cala Marina – 2016

Bernardo drove us back to town and dropped us off at Maria's townhouse, where her son Renzo was waiting for us. Maria, who is such a lovely and caring lady, insisted that I stay for dinner, which was a feast - homemade pasta, salad, grilled meat, potatoes and zucchini, plus many dolce. I kept closing my eyes while eating and Maria told Renzo that she thought I needed to dormire (sleep). I laughed and said that I was in heaven and savoring each bite. Nothing like homemade spaghetti, then dolce, berries and caffé normale.

A stupendous dinner!

Maria's Homemade Spaghetti – 2016

After talking and looking at photo albums, I decided to walk back to the B&B so I could begin to digest that wonderful meal. On the way, I stopped around the corner at the Villa Comunale and took some photos. What a wonderful day.

View of the Harbour in Castellammare del Golfo from the Villa Comunale

In and Around Castellammare del Golfo

The next morning, I arrived early at the Café Garibaldi and claimed a small table outside. As I was having my breakfast of caffè normale and a pistachio cornetto (to die for) and perusing my family chart, a small door to my right opened and a woman and two small children stepped out. I smiled at them but the woman looked at me and gave me the evil eye. I knew she was thinking, "Who the heck is she?" I smiled and laughed to myself; she had the same look that my sister Laurie had given me many years ago in Rome.

You need to understand that in small towns and villages, everyone knew each other. So, when a stranger appears in the town during off-season, the questions fly amongst the residents. The town had a population of approximately fifteen thousand people.

Before long the café became very busy. Two women were looking around for a place to sit, so I waved them over. They introduced themselves as Monika and Marne, a mother and daughter on a mini-vacation. I said, "No, you must be sisters?" They laughed and said they have heard that many times. I learned that Marne, the daughter, works with refugees in northern Italy. Her mom, Monika, is French, married an Austrian and divorced. They asked why I was there. I showed them my genealogy chart and the whole family history book. I explained that

I was meeting new cousins, exploring the family hometown and doing more research. They were fascinated. Marne said she knew nothing of her father's family and maybe she should start asking questions. After breakfast, we said goodbye and they were off to hike in the Zingaro Reserve.

Soon after, Cousin Bernardo tracked me down and said, "Andiamo." He decided that it was time to go for a drive and told the family we would be gone all day.

We headed east and drove through the countryside for about an hour. Along the way, we saw rows of olive trees, vineyards, and beautiful green mountains. It was absolutely breathtaking. Bernardo said we were going to the town of Monreale, specifically to see the Cattedrale di Monreale, a Norman cathedral known for its bronze doors and mosaic bible scenes. The road leading into the town was beginning to get narrow, so much so that it really looked like a one-way road. We parked in a parking garage, which I was shocked to see, and began our walk, along with many other people, into town through the winding cobblestoned streets. I could feel the anticipation in the air.

As the foot traffic eased a little, I saw an open space ahead. Turning my head to the left, I saw the Cattedrale piazza with a beautiful fountain. Then I saw the outside architecture of the Cattedrale, including the bell tower, which was magnificent. As we continued walking, we finally reached the entrance and saw two workers who were cleaning and restoring the outside mosaic. There are no words nor photos that give it justice.

Unbelievably gorgeous!

First View of the Cattedrale – 2016

Fountain in Front of Cattedrale – 2016

Restoring and Cleaning the Facade of Cattedrale – 2016

Cattedrale di Monreale

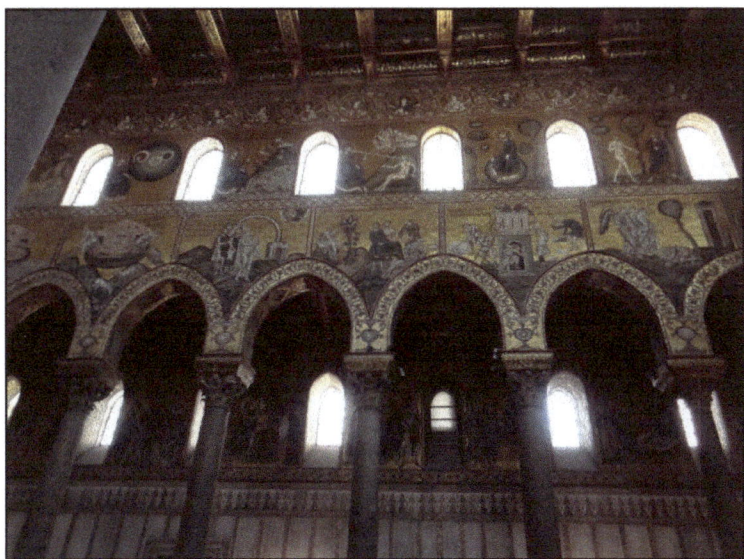

Afterwards, we walked around the town for a short time but Bernardo wanted to continue on to Palermo where he wanted to show me one or two sites. Thankfully, he knew how to deal with the Palermo traffic and found a parking space.

We first stopped to see the Capuchin Catacombs, which were originally built to bury monks from the local monastery. No photos were allowed. Visiting there was incredible and heart wrenching at the same time. To see row after row of adults, children and babies (mummified or skeletons) dressed in burial clothes was unreal. They lay in stacked glass boxes, open coffins and on shelves without coverings. Those images will stay burned in my mind forever. That's all I can say.

Bernardo also brought me to see the Theatre Massimo. It opened in May 1897 as an opera house but closed in 1974 for twenty-three years to be refurbished. It re-opened in 1997. We were only able to access the foyer area but it was impressively beautiful.

Foyer of Teatro Massimo – 2016

Afterwards, we walked around town and then decided it was time to eat. We had a wonderful lunch at Spinnato on Via Principe di Belmonte, 111, in Palermo. I had a spinach rice cake, ice tea and of course, a sfogliatelle, which was a shell-shaped flaky pastry filled with ricotta. You all know what I'm talking about. The sfogliatelle was delicious – the best I ever had.

My senses were on overload as we continued walking and absorbing the sights and sounds of Palermo. Bernardo was always listening to other conversations and when he heard English being spoken, he always interrupted and made the introductions, including my being from America. We met many people that day but the family that I most remember was a young American family on vacation before going on their next Navy assignment.

Wow, another action-packed day!

But I did miss walking around Castellammare del Golfo. So, later that night I took a walk which led me to Mama Cocha's Restaurant for a delicious late-night snack – an outrageous small personal pizza. Mama Cocha's was a wonderful restaurant, two corners from Maria's house and directly across from the Villa Comunale. It had both indoor and outdoor seating.

But who wants to sit inside?

When it was chilly at night, they had small lap blankets to keep you warm while eating. And of course, right after, I went next door to Vernaci, for a scoop of gelato.

It doesn't get any better. Another exciting day in Sicily!

Gelato at Vernaci's – 2016

Mama Sanfilippo

Cousin Bernardo tracked me down, where else? On the Corso Garibaldi! He said "Andiamo, Let's go. You are going to meet the Sanfilippo family." I smiled and my mind wandered.

Ahhh! Two years ago, during one of our Skype phone calls, Bernardo said one of his childhood friends lived in Florida. I chuckled as he was always telling me. "I know someone in New York City and his name is…." I tried to tell Bernardo that more than likely I wouldn't know this person. So, I asked, "What is the town." Much to my amazement, he said "Sebastian." Sebastian! That's the next town north of me. So, he gave me the contact information, I called and introduced myself and we made plans to meet for lunch – Vito Sanfilippo, his wife Pauline, my Vito and me. We had a wonderful time at Mulligan's Beach House, overlooking the Indian River Lagoon.

Ironically, last year, while my husband Vito and I were having dinner at a local restaurant, Counter Culture, we were very loud and laughing with the owner Chef Anthony Damiano. I looked across the room and mouthed "Sorry" to a young couple.

After dinner, they came over to the table and wanted to speak with Anthony. The young woman said, "With a name like Vito you can't be bad. My Dad's name is Vito." As we continued talking and laughing, all the towns that our families were from were mentioned. When the town of Castellammare del Golfo was mentioned, my mind was going at warp speed. I asked the young woman, "Is your Dad, Vito Sanfilippo, from Castellammare and a friend of my cousin Bernardo?" She and I were both stunned. Nina knew all about my cousin. Unreal.

"Andiamo, stop daydreaming," Bernardo said again. We left and drove to his home, stopped in to say "Ciao" to his wife, Vincenza and then walked over to meet the family. Bernardo introduced me to everyone and then left. He did not tell me I was invited to lunch! Had I known, I would have brought a bottle of wine!!

Giuseppina, Vito's sister, was the hostess and had made a feast for lunch – pasta with meat sauce, salad, scrumptious olive bread, fresh olives, tender chicken cutlets, fruit, and dolce. It was like my childhood when everyone was eating, talking, gesturing, and laughing, all at the same time! Of course, my lack of language came into play but Giuseppina's grandchildren practiced their English with me. No need for the dictionary, yet.

The one person who remained calm during the entire afternoon was Mama Nina Sanfilippo. She had a quiet grace that surrounded her. I can't think of another way to say it.

While having caffé normale, I asked permission to take some photos for Pauline and Vito back home. The only person I did not photograph was Ercole, Vito's brother, as he left right after lunch, which upset his mother very much.

Soon after, I was asked if I could walk Mama home across the street so she could rest. No problem. As I took her arm, I could feel she was still steaming mad and trembling. When we arrived, she changed her shoes and gestured let's go. Mama had other ideas and resting was not one of them. Deep in my heart, I knew where we were headed. We walked with our arms wrapped around each other, as I didn't want her to falter.

When we arrived at Ercole's home, we knocked and as he opened the door, I could see that he was shocked. He looked up and down the street for a car but I said, "No macchina. Abbiamo camminato, No car, we walked." I thought he was going to faint. He quickly directed his mother to a big comfortable chair in the living room.

After I was introduced to Ercole's wife and children and took a tour of their home, Mama Nina insisted we take photos. She was a funny and stubborn lady. I had a lot of fun especially when I brought out my dictionary!

Fast forward to August 2, 2017. I was very sad to see the Facebook posts by Nina and her sister Danielle saying a sad farewell to Mama Nina. In the short time I spent with her, I found her to be a very caring, loving, funny and special woman. "A presto Mama."

Gentlemen of Castellammare del Golfo

Word had spread that my parenti (family) was from Castellammare del Golfo and I was researching my roots. Every morning, I met, spoke, mimed or Google translated with many people at the Café. They were curious and wanted to see my family tree chart.

When some of the older gentlemen learned that I was born in New York City, the stories began. Many worked in the New York, Pennsylvania and New Jersey area and enjoyed speaking to me in English, as it had been awhile since they spoke it. I learned that some were "seasonal commuters," as they came to America to work as needed, whether it be in construction, marble or the mines. If they were good workers the boss would tell them to come back by a certain date and if they knew of any other good workers, bring them along. Others stayed in America, sent money home and would occasionally go back home to visit. I had many enjoyable conversations with them.

"My table" at Café Garibaldi grew and some mornings we put two or three tables together. Both my family history book and chart would be spread out and people would peruse it and point to the ones they knew. It was surreal. I would hear, "Ah, Lorenzo. È la cugina di cui ha parlato. (Ah Lorenzo. She is the cousin he spoke about.)"

On one particular morning when I arrived at the Café, the owner, Vito Alfano, greeted me and we sat outside. A little while later, I was joined by a gentleman, Enzo, who was a wonderful man and childhood friend of my cousin Bernardo.

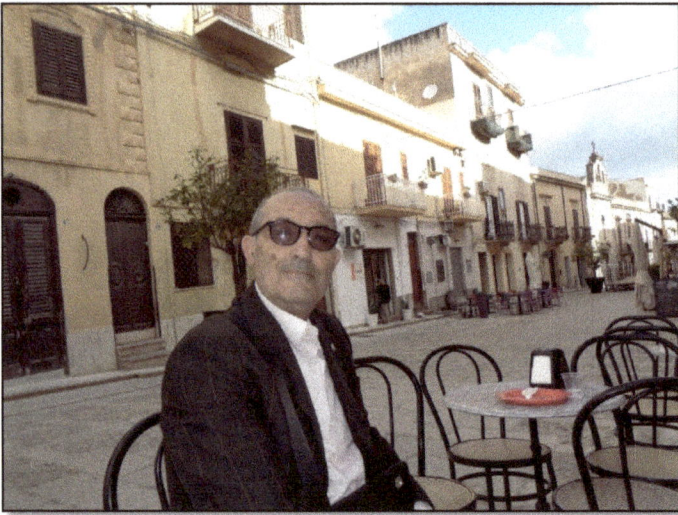

Enzo – 2016

Enzo was a retired IT (Information Technology) professor and City Commissioner. When I told him that I was a retired mainframe computer programmer and web designer, we both laughed. We had a very enjoyable morning discussing tech. He also asked to see the charts and book I had, as people had told him why I was here. I laughed again, as I was born in New York City and brought up in the Bronx and Yonkers, where everyone did not know your name nor your family.

Two Great-Grandfathers

I had many goals for that trip, but the most important one was to find additional information about two great-grandfathers - Giuseppe Maria Vivona, a barber and Lorenzo Milano, a shoemaker. Both had been born in the mountain town of Calatafimi and had found their way to the small fishing village of Castellammare del Golfo, eleven miles away.

Information about my Great-Grandfather Vivona had been very elusive, and a question had been buzzing around in my head for many years, "Dove sei Giuseppe Maria Vivona? (Where is Giuseppe Maria Vivona?)"

Great-Grandparents Giuseppe Maria Vivona and Angelina Giliberti
Vivona.
Photo courtesy of K. Vega and D. Veit.

I had been searching for any information about him for two decades
and had found nothing about him after 1908 when his last child was
born.

How can that be?

The Vivona pedigree chart follows as well as additional
information I found through research.

Giuseppe VIVONA Married:Calatafimi, Trapani, Sicily	**Catherina DI MATTEA**	**Joseph CATALANO**	**Francesca (UNKNOWN)**

Francesco VIVONA
Married: 9 Oct 1746 Calatafimi, Trapani, Sicily

Josepha CATALANO

Giuseppe VIVONA
Died: bef 1805 Calatafimi, Trapani, Sicily; Married: 8 Jan 1775 Calatafimi,

Maria GIORINTANO [GIURINTANO]

Rosario Pasquale Maianus VIVONA Born: 7 Jul 1777 Calatafimi, Trapani, Sicily; Married: 8	**Francesca LEONARDO**	**Salvatore INTERNICOLA**	**Margarita AGNECI**

Michele Maria Gaetano VIVONA
Born: 21 Nov 1808 Calatafimi, Trapani, Sicily; Married: 12

Giuseppa INTERNICOLA
Born: 1809

Salvatore VIVONA
Born: 24 Oct 1839; Married: 30 Apr 1862 Calatafimi, Trapani, Sicily

Agostina BOLENA

Giuseppe Maria VIVONA
Born: 29 May 1865 Calatafimi, Sicily; Died: 1910

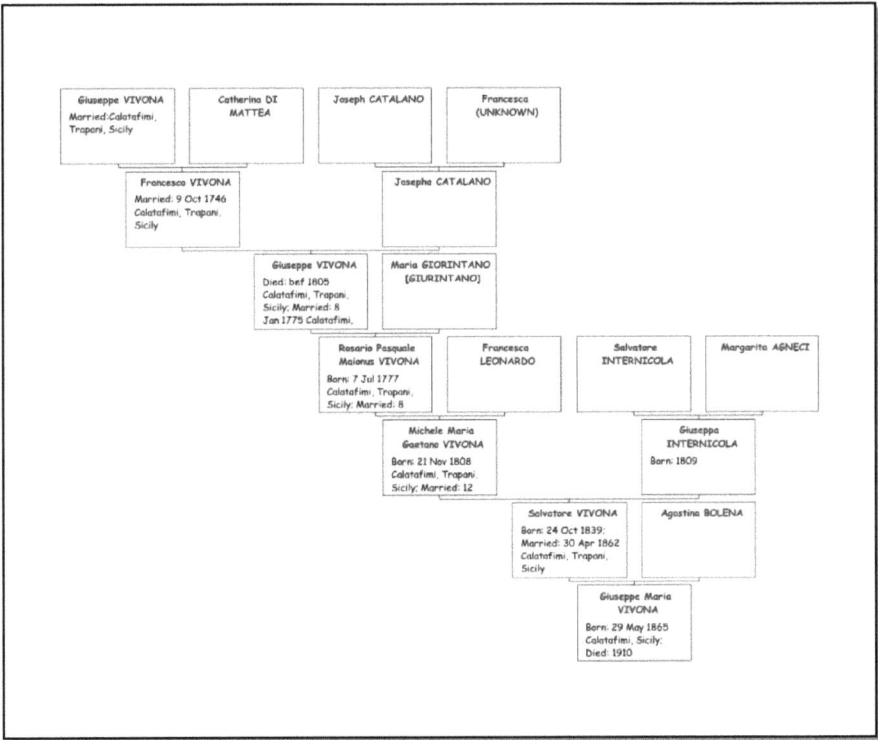

As indicated on the pedigree chart, he was the son of Salvatore VIVONA and Agostina BOLENA and was born in May 1865 in Calatafimi, Trapani, Sicily. He was baptized the same day in the San Giuliano Church by the priest Giuseppe Orlando. His godparents were Giorgio and Francesca Scianna. His occupation was a barber/surgeon. The occupation information was in a letter that belonged to my Cousin Betty Palumbo's mother, Elisabetta, his youngest daughter. Betty was kind enough to give me a copy.

Giuseppe Maria Vivona married Angelina Giliberti, who was born in Castellammare del Golfo in July 1867. She was the daughter of Michele and Girolama LaTorre. Giuseppe and Angelina were married on November 13, 1889 at San Giuliano Parish in Calatafimi, Trapani, Sicily. They lived in Castellammare del Golfo and had the following children:

Salvatore VIVONA – born May 1891

Maria VIVONA – born August 1894 – married Antonino Bongiorno in CdelG Jan 1912

Michele VIVONA – born and died the same day in May 1896

Michele VIVONA – born May 1897 – married Anna Frazzitta in Palermo May 1921

Girolama VIVONA – born January 1899

Rosaria VIVONA – born April 1901

Giuseppe Maria Umberto VIVONA – born February 1906

Elisabetta VIVONA – born in July 1908

∞∞∞∞

Angelina Giliberti Vivona, my great-grandmother, immigrated into the Port of New York with her daughters Giroloma (age fourteen) and Elisabetta (age five) on September 30, 1913, aboard the ship SS Canada. Angelina was listed as a widow on the manifest. Two other children, Rosaria and Giuseppe, followed afterwards. Angelina died in November 1928 at the age of sixty-one at Harlem Hospital in New York City.

So, what happened to my great-grandfather Giuseppe Maria Vivona?

I had to assume that he died in Sicily, as the ship manifest indicated. To be thorough, I searched the files on the Ellis Island website without success.

Did he immigrate elsewhere?

Through research, I discovered that many women who immigrated listed themselves as widows when not traveling with a male family member.

So, did he really die in Sicily or did he live his life elsewhere apart from his family?

I also checked census records and the city directories for New York City, but to no avail. It was driving me nuts. I mentioned this to Cousin Bernardo and said it was time for me to go to the Stato Civile in Calatafimi to speak with the clerk, Signora Serafina Cataldo, who has helped me via snail mail in the past. I also wanted to ask her about a birth record she'd recently sent me.

When we arrived, I checked in at the reception desk and sat down to wait. Meanwhile, Bernardo chatted with everyone and I kept hearing him say "America." He was on his rant, once again, about how I was here from America researching our family history but did not speak Italian. By then I had the impression that the word had gone out that an American was in the building. Why? Because as Bernardo and I were waiting in line to speak with Signora Cataldo, a Facebook friend, Signor Salvo Mucaria, came running down the stairs.

I had texted him prior to my trip but didn't say when I would be in Calatafimi. It was a pleasure to finally meet him. Signor Salvo Mucaria, in addition to his friend Signor Rosario Vivona, posted many photos and histories of Calatafimi and its people. A truly wonderful project.

Calatafimi terra ricca di tradizioni, storia e orgogliosociale on Facebook
https://www.facebook.com/groups/calatafimi/

When my name was called, I went into the clerk's office and introduced myself. I was so happy to hear, "Ah, signora, sono Serafina Cataldo e sono io che ho risposto a tutte le vostre richieste. (Ah signora, I am Serafina Cataldo and I am the one who has been responding to all your requests.)" We were happy to finally meet each other in person.

Signor Salvo Mucaria and Signora Serafina Cataldo in the Stato Civile
in Calatafimi – 2016

Before leaving the U.S., I wrote down my questions regarding both binonnos (great-grandfathers) in Italian. I didn't want to take the chance that my miming and attempts to speak were misunderstood.

My first request was for any additional information about Giuseppe M. Vivona. Signora Cataldo, climbed the tall library ladder and pulled a registry book, but other than his birth and marriage information, there was no other annotation. He didn't die in Calatafimi. Rats!

Next, I had a copy of the birth record for Lorenzo Milano that Signora Cataldo had recently sent to me, in addition to my list of questions. The Signora reviewed both documents. She asked why I had a question about the birth document. I said it did not state his parenti (parents). The Signora nodded, rolled the ladder to the high cabinet, and climbed. I held the ladder for her and took the book she handed down. She opened the book to the index, found his name, and went to the page. His name was listed but no parents. She went to another page and perused it, shook her head and looked sad. Then she explained to us that he had been "left at the wheel," abbandonato (abandoned). Cousin Bernardo looked like he was going to faint, as he had no knowledge of this. I felt very sad for my great-grandfather Lorenzo and wondered what kind of childhood he'd had. He was born in 1862, two years after the Battle of Calatafimi, which had been fought between Giuseppe Garibaldi's Freedom Fighters and the troops of the Kingdom of Two Sicilies. The island of Sicily had been in turmoil.

Signora Cataldo was very kind and allowed me to take photos of the page. At the time, not all records were digitized, so, unless you visited the Stato Civile in the Comune, those records were lost to you. We stayed for about three hours and thanked the Signora for all that she did for us.

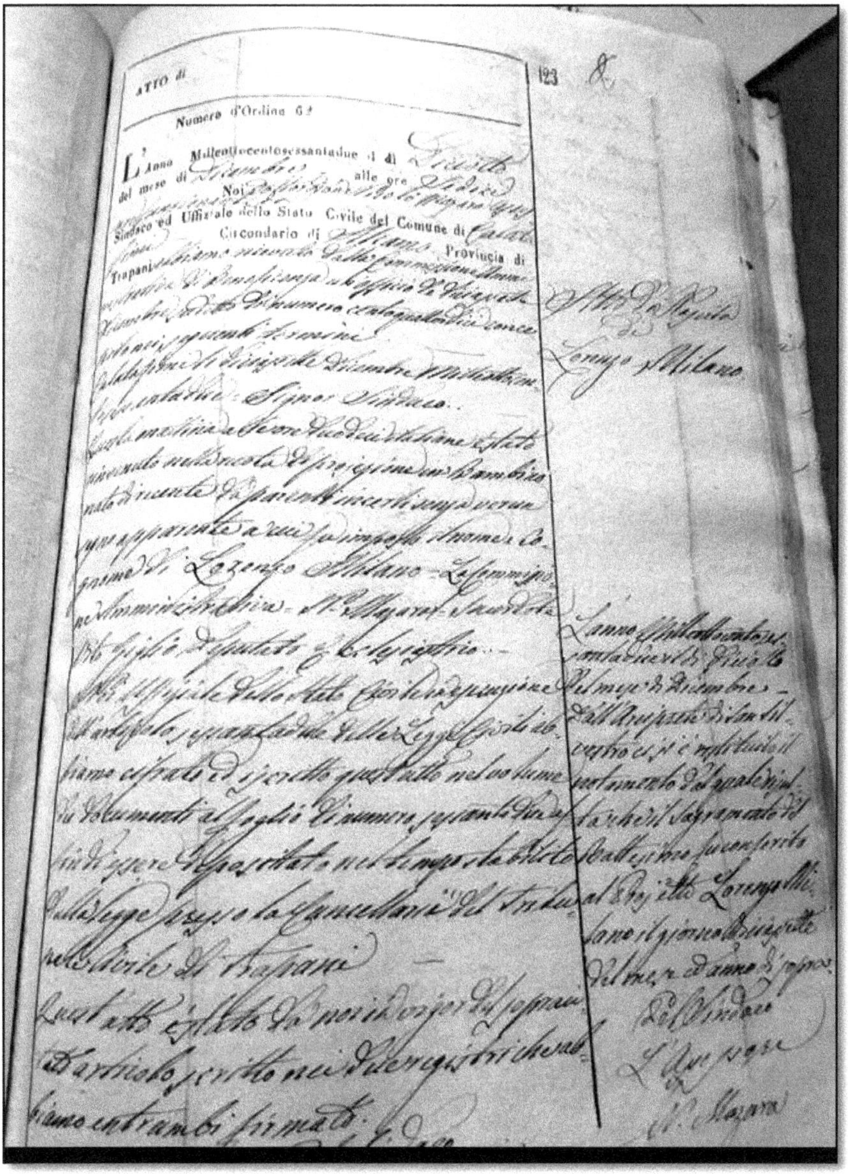

While in Calatafimi...

`

After leaving Signora Cataldo and the Stato Civile, Bernardo and I walked around the mountain town. It is surreal to walk the same streets that my great-grandfathers had walked. We absorbed all the sights and sounds of everyday life. We saw some awesome things - the churches, the side streets, and even the vegetable vendors. But all I wanted to do was roam the streets, see the people and listen to the dialect being spoken. Plus, I really enjoyed the atmosphere and the smell of the fresh mountain air, which I missed after leaving Colorado many decades ago.

A Calatafimi Veggie Vendor – 2016

Chiesa del Santissimo Crocifisso in Calatafimi – 2016

Chiesa Della Vergine del Soccorso o Chiesella – 2016

As we were strolling along, we found the Headquarters and House of Giuseppe Garibaldi, a leader in the reunification of Italy. We went in for a tour.

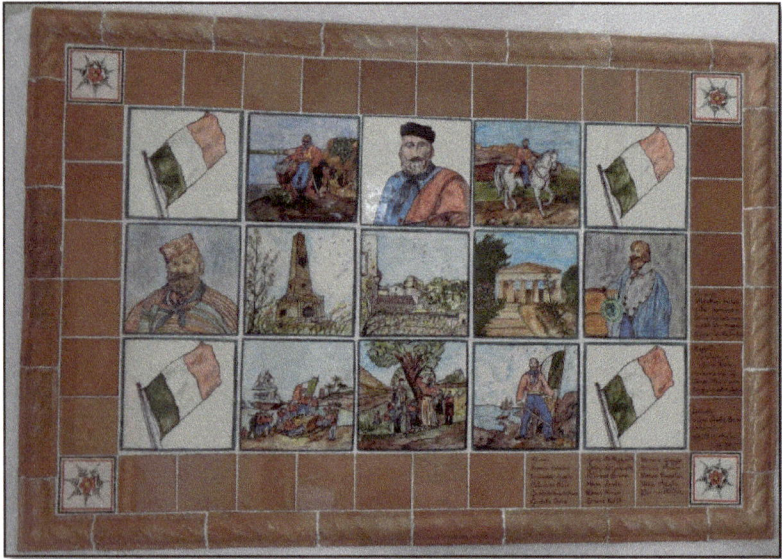

Casa Garibaldi plaque and entry foyer in Garibaldi's house – 2016

After another hour or so, Bernardo again said, "Andiamo. I have another place to show you." As we drove up into the mountainous countryside around Calatafimi, a camper was coming down the mountain road. Bernardo waved his arm out the window and the camper stopped. My cousin was always doing this. So, then he and the other driver, who was from Germany where Bernardo lived, carried on a conversation from the vehicles – for about a half hour. While this was going on, I watched the cattle graze, took photos of the flowers, and enjoyed the peace.

The only reason Bernardo and the other driver stopped talking was because another car was trying to get down the mountain. We continued our drive up to our destination, Ossario di Pianto Romano. It was a spectacular monument on the hill, a tribute to all the young partisans, known as Garibaldi's Freedom Fighters, who fought the Bourbon soldiers during the 1860 Battle of Calatafimi. It was the beginning of the unification of Italy.

I had recently read the book "My Life" by Giuseppe Garibaldi, where he tells the story of the origins of the freedom fighters and their journey. It was a great book, which gave me insight into what had been happening in Sicily when all of my great-grandparents were born.

Ossario in Calatafimi – 2016

Ossario in Calatafimi – 2016

Inside wall plaque of those buried in the Ossario in Calatafimi – 2016

I was surprised that Bernardo took me there, as he had been complaining for days that I spent too much time at the cemetery and inquiring into records for our ancestors. But he just didn't understand my need, or yes, maybe my obsession, to find information about my great-grandfather, Giuseppe.

Also, from the vantage point of the monument, I was able to take a panoramic photo of the entire town of Calatafimi.

The day after our excursion to Calatafimi, I saw my friend Enzo for our morning caffè normale. I had mentioned to him the "brick walls" of genealogy research and how it can be very challenging and frustrating, especially finding information concerning my great-grandfather. He recommended going to la Biblioteca (the library) and ask to see the city directories.

I didn't mention this to Bernardo, but early one morning, before going for my morning caffé normale, I walked to la Biblioteca by myself. After being buzzed in and signing the register, I spoke with a young librarian. I told her I was looking for any information regarding my great-grandfather, showed her the information I had and said that I didn't care if he had many wives and other children. She laughed and said it was very possible. She then told the archivist, who looked through records from 1908 until 1935 but found no entry for Giuseppe Maria Vivona.

So, where the heck is he?

I have written many letters to those with the surname Vivona in and around Castellammare del Golfo, Calatafimi, New York and New Jersey, but no one has any information about him.

Newly found cousins in north Florida have been gracious in providing me photos of our great-grandmother Angelina and her children. Plus, Cousin Kim and Cousin Dede provided the photo of the painting of Angelina and Giuseppe, the only likeness I have of him. It is my hope that one day, before I die, I can visit his grave.

Locating the Grave of Great-Grandfather Lorenzo Milano

Great-Grandfather Lorenzo Milano Grave Marker – 2016

Then came the day that Cousin Maria was going to show us where our great-grandfather Lorenzo Milano was buried. Yes, I know to those non-genealogists this is a little strange but to family genealogists, it's a wonderful thing.

Bernardo and I had been to the cemetery four times and had not been able to locate the grave. We'd looked above ground at the mausoleums, graves, crypts and below ground in the catacombs. But I remembered seeing the grave and it was in a mausoleum wall. We even went to the office to inquire, but there was no information. Nada. How was that possible? I had Signor Cassara check several books. I also had him check for my other great-grandfather, Giuseppe Maria Vivona.

Nothing.

I could've kicked myself; seventeen years ago, when Cousin Lorenzo brought Laurie and me to the cemetery, we saw the grave. I even took notes of each grave that we visited. I wasn't bold enough to take photos at that time, but I have since learned to do so.

Notes Lorenzo Milano great grandfa
12-8-1935 morto
77 ys old
Ripulsero nella vita
laboriosa e Corretta
di milano Lorenzo

Bernardo picked me up and we drove to Cousin Maria's home, where we had caffé normale. We then piled into the car and drove to the "Cimitero Comunale" on the other side of town. Maria reminded us that each week she changed the flowers at his grave.

Once we arrived, Maria, who is tiny at 4'10", moved quickly through the cemetery and went to the mausoleum wall I'd been looking at. She located and rolled over one of those huge "library" ladders. Then she climbed up and all I could do was hold her and the ladder. Bernardo fetched water and then I handed Maria the flowers. And there it was (outlined in blue).

Mausoleum wall where our great-grandfather Lorenzo Milano rests
2016

No wonder I couldn't see it. For those of you who know me, I am vertically challenged, a.k.a. short, plus the inscription on the stone had faded. No way did it look like the stone I saw many years ago.

Grave Marker for Great-Grandfather Lorenzo Milano in Cimitero Comunale (Via Euclide, Castellammare Del Golfo) – 2016

I couldn't thank Maria enough. After paying our respects, we went with Maria to her husband's, my cousin Lorenzo's, mausoleum standalone house. We swept out the dust, watered the plants, changed the water in all the vases and added fresh cut flowers. We also visited all the other family graves.

The office was closed when we were leaving but when I returned home to the U.S., I wrote to Signor Maurizio Cassara inquiring into the process and cost to clean and restore my great-grandfather's grave marker. As of this writing, I had yet to hear from him. More on that later.

A Great Day – Café Garibaldi and San Vito Lo Capo

Corso Garibaldi – 2016

One morning, much to my surprise, I found two older gentlemen sitting at "my" table in Café Garibaldi. After greetings, the first man asked if I spoke Italian. I shook my head and said unfortunately no. He then introduced himself as Leonardo Galatioto and the other man as his brother Felice. Leonardo was a retired police officer, who spoke some English. He told me that they had heard that my parenti came from Castellammare del Golfo and that I had a chart that showed their surnames. He then asked to see it, so I showed them the Galatioto branch of the chart. They were amazed and excited by the amount of information I had gathered: births, baptisms, marriages, deaths, immigration, stories passed along, and more. Plus, when they saw the photos, they were surprised to see my cousin Lorenzo, who had recently passed away. They were friends of Lorenzo. They hugged and kissed me but did not say if they were of the same Galatioto family. The brothers then mentioned that their sister lived in Floral Park, NY. Before long, my friend Enzo and Bernardo joined us for caffé normale and also perused the chart.

Note: My grandfather Rosario Milano's mother was Anna Galatioto, daughter of Rosario Galatioto and Catherine Sceusa. I had to wonder if they were of Leonardo's lineage. In addition, I'd recently received a copy of my parents' New York City marriage record, which showed a Rosario "Roy" Galatioto as Dad's best man.

After the brothers and Enzo left, Bernardo had a surprise for me. We hopped into the car and drove west for thirty miles or so, to the beautiful seaside town of San Vito Lo Capo.

I had previously mentioned to Bernardo that I wanted to go back to the town that my sister and I had enjoyed many years ago. It was beautiful there and very relaxing. It had larger cobblestone streets, that gave the town a very open feeling – and it had a killer view. We sauntered around the town looking in all the little shops, went to the beach, and spoke to many folks along the way, including a couple and their daughter from Tennessee.

We finally found our way to the church, Santuario San Vito Lo Capo, where I took some photos inside. After having more caffé normale, we headed back home.

Another great day of exploring!

Inside the Santuario (Church) in San Vito Lo Capo – 2016

My Last Full Day in Sicily

I don't know why but I woke up very early with a need to check my phone. In addition to a horrendous thunderstorm, a tornado hit Vero Beach on May 17, 2016. I called Vito to make sure he was okay. He said he was but that all the roads were flooded, including ours, and people were stranded in their cars.

Yikes!

After that upsetting phone call, I pulled myself together and headed towards the Corso for a cappuccino and a tort at Café Cucece. Why there? Café Garibaldi was closed that day. While I was out, I bought some sweets for Maria for dessert later in the day. I also checked on the ongoing renovation project diagonally across from the Café.

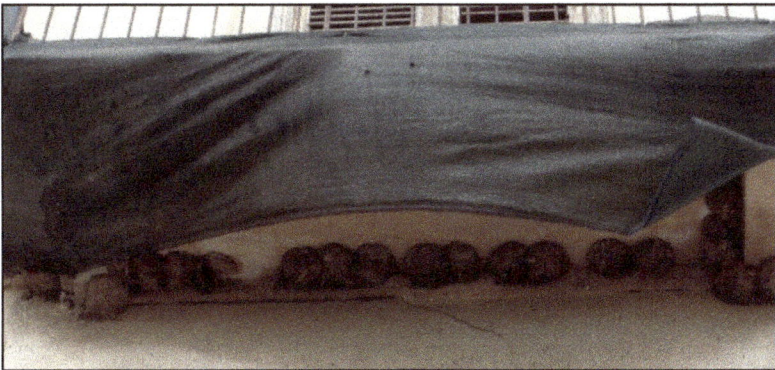

The previous morning, workers had been removing swallow's nests from under the balconies, which I thought was horrendous. Couldn't they have waited until the nesting season was over? So, that morning it was very sad to hear all the screeching and see the swallows still flying around looking for their nests.

After breakfast, I walked around one last time, down the Corso Garibaldi, which turned into Via Giacomo Puccini. I walked over the bridge to the castle and took more photos. Afterward, I walked back up the stairs and over to Piazza Europa, to the fruit vendor for strawberries. Then I wandered over to Piazza Petrolo to watch the waves of the Tyrrhenian Sea roll up the beach.

Looping around, I went shopping for a few souvenirs along Via Giacomo Puccini and found a great shop, Sikelia Sicilian Souvenirs, and met its young owners, Leonardo and Cristina. Leonardo explained to me that his grandmother had started the shop, and he was carrying on the family tradition. He asked why I was in town, so I explained I was meeting new cousins and researching the family history. He asked me the family surnames, of which he knew a few. His mother's surname was Ciaravino, which was Cousin Maria's maiden name. I asked if they were related. He said, "No, but we are all related, no?" Smart man.

I continued my walk to Maria's house for lunch with her and Cousin Renzo – macaroni with zucchini sauce and tomatoes, grilled potatoes and lamb, cookies and fruit (cheeso) including peaches and arance (oranges).

To absolutely die for!

While eating the homemade pasta, I closed my eyes as I was enjoying it immensely. Maria thought I needed to sleep; dormire was what I heard again. I laughed because it was a running joke. Again, I told Renzo to please tell Maria that lunch was wonderful. I was in heaven, savoring every bite.

Too funny!

I stayed a few hours, as Maria showed me another one of her photo albums. By then I knew who some of the folks were in Grandma Rosaria's photos that I inherited from Dad and Mom. As I left, hugging and kissing Maria, I said, "A presto. (See you soon.)"

Renzo and I walked to my favorite spot, the Villa Comunale, where we said, "See you again soon," and then parted. I called Vito, took more photos there and others along the way back to the B&B where Felice was waiting for me. He had texted me that he would pick me up the next morning at 5:15 a.m., as at that time the traffic to the airport would be very light. His parents came by to say, "Buongiornato. (Good journey.)," as did my cousin Elena. I hadn't seen them for a few days, as they were all sick with a virus.

By 8:00 p.m., I was out again walking, this time to Vernaci's where a gelato had my name on it. Afterwards, back at the B&B with a heavy heart, I packed, set the alarm, and tried to sleep – but it didn't happen.

123

The Flight Home

I was up at 3:30 a.m. so I would be ready by 5:15. Felice was driving me to the Falcone Borsellino Airport in Palermo, formerly known as the Punta Raisi Airport. When we arrived at the airport at 6:00 a.m., we hugged, kissed, and said, "A presto." I checked my luggage and went through TSA in no time. On the quick flight to Rome, I had a caffé normale and cornetto.

I arrived in Rome, went through TSA (Yes again) and passport control, then I trekked to the farthest international terminal, of course. Once I arrived at the Alitalia gate, I checked on my seat assignment and waited to board the flight to Miami. A little while later, there was an announcement of a delay due to a strike of the French air traffic controllers.

Really?

Now, those of you who have traveled know all about these strikes, especially in Europe. They can be a pain in the butt and cause all kinds of travel nightmares. As I waited, with another caffé normale, I thought of the time my younger sister, Sarah, and I went to the Seville Expo, eons ago. The day of our return to NY, via Madrid to JFK, there was a strike by Spanair in Malaga. We had to re-book our flights and unfortunately had to stay in Torremolinos on the beach, another two days, which was a very big inconvenience. Vito laughed when I called him to ask him to notify my boss and tell her the news.

Mmmmm....maybe an extra day or two in Rome isn't a bad idea. I have cousins in Rome.

Two hours later, an announcement was made stating that the Spanish air traffic controllers would be taking over and we could board. Way too ironic. Once everyone had settled and Alitalia turned on the in-flight entertainment, I turned to my favorite news channel, BBC. That's when I heard that Egypt Air Flight MS804 had crashed into the eastern Mediterranean Sea.

Mother have mercy!

All you could hear around the plane were gasps, except for a young couple sitting across from me who were still complaining about the delay. When I told them what happened, they just continued bitching. I said, "Stop complaining. It could've been you," and they finally shut up. I thought of the time that Vito and I flew to Rome on 9/18, a week after 9/11.

After an uneventful flight, the plane finally arrived safely in Miami.

Yes!

But then I had a three-hour trek home.

Imagine My Surprise

Whenever I ordered flowers for delivery in Sicily, I used the online Italian florist, Maria Fiorista. Not only did I always receive email delivery notifications, but they also informed me about the recipient, such as: whether the person was home, visiting someone, at the doctor or not feeling well. At the time, I was waiting for notification that Cousin Maria had received my flowers for November 2nd, All Souls Day. It was a tradition on this day to visit the graveyard to pay tribute to those of our family who had died. I know Maria visits each of our family graves, and I wanted to contribute flowers. I didn't receive notification from the florist but I did get a surprise when I saw an email from Salvatore Milano.

Really?

How did he obtain my email address? His mom and brother, Renzo, don't use computers although Cousin Felice does....hmmm.

Salvatore, whom I had yet to meet, was the youngest son of Cousin Maria and Lorenzo. He introduced himself by stating that he lived in Pisa, had a construction business and two sons, Lorenzo and Juri. Salvatore told me that we missed each other at the airport in May.

What?

I left early in the morning, and he had arrived early that afternoon. No one had mentioned to me that Salvatore was on his way to visit. Had I known, I would have changed my flight.

Salvatore wanted to thank me for the two copies of the Milano Family History book I left at his mom's house. He'd read through it and had some corrections. Over a series of emails, I mentioned that the information was obtained from his dad, Lorenzo, through several letters, which I attached to the email. Salvatore was happy that I'd corresponded with his dad who contributed to my knowledge of the family.

127

He also informed me that his brother, Renzo, was having health issues and was in the hospital. I asked if Maria needed help and if so, I would travel back to Sicily. As our correspondence continued, I learned that Renzo underwent successful heart surgery and has similar heart issues as my dad, Lorenzo (a.k.a. Larry), my sisters Laurie and Sarah, my brother Roy and myself. It still surprises me that unknown family members halfway across the world are still linked via DNA.

During our "conversations," I mentioned that my grandmother Rosaria Vivona Milano, his great-aunt-in-law, had many photos that I had inherited. I sent several to him electronically. Salvatore was astonished that I had the photos, especially ones of his father as a young boy and man, that he had never seen.

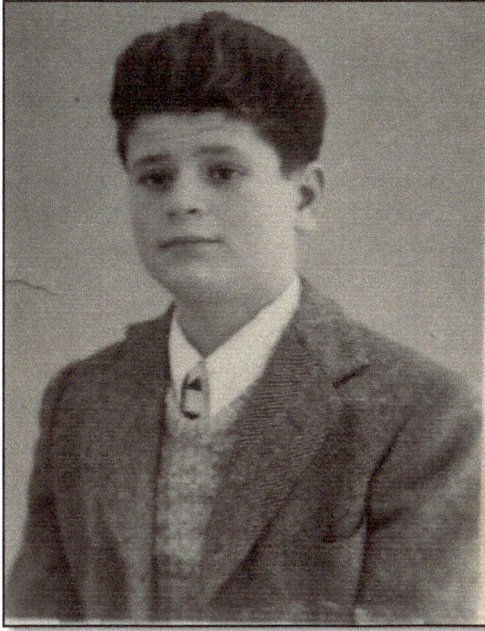

Another one of the photos I sent was of his Aunt Lucia as a young woman. I mentioned that Cousin Bernardo had said it was too far to drive to Gela. I had wanted to meet the family I just learned about during my trip. Sadly, a week after Salvatore received the photo, he wrote telling me she had just passed away. He forwarded the funeral information, so I sent flowers to the family in Gela.

Also, I told Salvatore the highlights of my trip and what I'd learned of the family history during my visits to Castellammare del Golfo and Calatafimi. He was astonished and sad to learn that our great-grandfather was "left at the wheel," abandoned at birth. So, what does this mean? The FamilySearch.org website explains "Italian Infant Abandonment" better than I could.

"...new mothers anonymously abandoned their infants at la ruota (the wheel) located in the outside wall of the ospizio (hospital) sometimes leaving segno di riconoscimento (a sign of recognition) such as the image of a saint, a foreign coin, a torn piece of cloth, or other talisman, to preserve the mother's ability, rarely exercised, of returning to reclaim the child, sometimes a year later or even many years later."

https://www.familysearch.org/wiki/en/Italian_Infant_Abandonment

Photo of wheel provided by Daniele Giurintano, Calatafimi 2017

He also didn't know that his mother had to show Bernardo and me the grave because we couldn't find it, due to the deterioration of the gravestone. So now, the grave of our great-grandfather Lorenzo Milano became the main topic of our correspondence.

January 25, 2017
Celia to Salvatore:

I am hoping that you can help me solve this issue.
Several times Bernardo & I went to the cemetery in May & I could not find our great-grandfather's grave. I knew it was in a mausoleum but could not remember where your Father took Laurie & me many years ago.

Your mom said she would show us & she did. When I saw the tombstone, I knew why I couldn't find it. In addition to being vertically challenged (short), the stone was faded.
When I came home I wrote 2 times to Maurizio at the cemetery. He never answered me. I also asked Felice & I heard from him yesterday via facebook - "I lavori non li faràil Comune. Devi fare tuilavori, devipagaretu per illavoro. Work will not be done by the municipality. You have to do the work... you have to pay for the job."

How can I have the work done to restore the stone? And yes, I will pay the fees.
I am attaching the 2nd letter to the cemetery which includes the note to Maurizio.

January 25, 2017
Salvatore to Celia:

Hi Celia, I wanted to tell you that the work to fix the graves is done by relatives and not the municipality. With us it is so.

If you want to do the work inform me. In recent months, my mother told me that the city needs to release the posts and that there could be risk that they will exhume him and put him in the common ossuaries.

January 26, 2017
Celia to Salvatore:

Hi Salvatore, Thank you for all the information. Yes, is it possible to have the stone cleaned? Or should I wait until I visit to arrange it??

What does your mother mean by "the city needs to release the posts and that there could be risk that he will be exhumed and put in the common ossuaries." !@#$%^&*

Do I need to pay a fee to keep him where he is? If so, please let me know, as I will pay it. I have heard from people in my genealogy group that if fees are not paid, then the bones are dug up and put in a mass grave. Therefore no one knows where their ancestors are buried. I will NOT have that happen!

January 28, 2017
Salvatore to Celia:

Hi Celia, how are you? I hope you are fine. I'm going to be calling a person in Castellammare and I hope to know if it is better to clean the stone or to get a new stone. I'll try to do so but I don't live in Castellammare and it isn't easy planning. I hope to give you some news soon.

I don't know if is possible to pay a fee to keep grandfather there. I think it's a good idea to replace the headstone. If the municipality sees that there are relatives who are interested they will not take him away. I hope to give you more next week. Have a nice weekend.

January 29, 2017
Celia to Salvatore:

Hi Salvatore, Thank you!!

I would also think that the fact that your mother places flowers every week shows that the relatives care & are still living in town.

While I was in Castellammare, I met a gentleman who knew your father & knows Bernardo. We had caffé normale many mornings at Cafe Garibaldi. We have been corresponding via Facebook & his name is Enzo F.... Do you want me to ask him for guidance about this?? He may be able to give us more information as he lives in CdG.

January 29, 2017
Celia to Enzo (translated from Italian):

Hi Enzo, I hope you and your family are well. While I was in Sicily I tried to inquire about the process for cleaning up and restoring my great-grandfather's gravestone without success. Shortly after my return from Sicily, with my surprise, I received an email from my cousin Salvatore, whom I did not meet. I've been corresponding with him. I told him about the tombstone. He said it was up to the family to do the repairs. I said good, please let me know and I will make the payment. But he recently wrote to me and said the following: "my mother told me that the city needs to free up places and that there might be a risk that he will be put in a common ossuary."

Does this mean that they remove the bones in another tomb? I'm so upset! What can I do? Any guidance from you is so much appreciated. Celia p.s. Thank God for Google translate!

January 30, 2017
Enzo to Celia:

Dear Celia, As regards the question about the cleaning and restoration of the tombstone, the municipal law orders all owners maintenance of the graves that is, cleaning and restoring the tombstones. Presently, the Mayor has decided to deprive the bones of the deceased who have not been honored by relatives for a long time. Christian bones are deposited in a common ossuary. I think and suggest that we must anticipate the Mayor's decision and arrange the cleaning and replacement of the tombstone as soon as possible, hoping that by doing so and noting the maintenance the Mayor will not remove the bones. I think that you will be in Castellammare again this year and I will be honored to try to solve this problem together. I want to ask you if you have a picture of the gravestone and its coordinates to find it so I can make sure it is still in place. Happy to be helpful with my suggestions, I send you a warm greeting together with your loved ones.

January 31, 2017
Celia to Enzo:

Dear Enzo, I never received a reply from Maurizio from the cemetery. Is there a business in Castellammare doing this job? Celia

January 31, 2017
Enzo to Celia:

Dear Celia, today with the sun and the clear day without rain, I was at the cemetery. I had trouble finding the tomb. In any case I have been informed about the maintenance and cleaning of marble gravestones at the cemetery. The right way is to entrust it to the specialist company for these jobs. Only the specialist firm can do these jobs because it is registered with the municipality and is authorized to do all this. The path to follow is as follows: 1) Fill out a printed "form" that is already in my possession; 2) Make a deposit of Euro 25; 3) Make the stamp of execution by signing the Mayor; 4) Make a cost estimate by the specialist company and then let him do the job. So only the specialized firm and not the private citizen can do these jobs. As you need to start your work, you need your signature and identity document, I think it would be appropriate when you're in Castellammare to complete everything. One of the companies specializing in these works is just beside the cemetery, that is, the Fontana company. He is a very good professional and I think he should be entrusted with the job. A hug, Enzo

February 3, 2017
Salvatore to Celia:

Hello Celia, Today I spoke with Fontana and told me the price is 200 Euro for cleaning the gravestone. The price also includes the permit fee for communication to the municipality and a new vase for the flowers. I was hoping to also talk to the head of cimiteroma but these days he is not at work. I'm going to CdG on March 11. Kisses

February 4, 2017
Celia to Salvatore

Hi Salvatore, thank you so much for doing this. It is great news!! This past November, I exchanged $'s for Euro, so I have Euros. Please let me know where you want me to send them.

If you are able to speak to the head of the cemetery, please ask if he received my 2 letters. I understand that they are not responsible but if I did not have you to contact them and information from Enzo, I would not know what the procedure was—communication with municipality, Fontana, etc.

Ah, your Mother's birthday. Both she & my sister Laurie were born on March 10th.

Have a wonderful Sunday!! Kisses!

February 4, 2017
Salvatore to Celia:

Hi Celia, I'm going to go to Castellammare just for my mother's birthday. It's incredible your sister was born the same day.

I told Fontana I will give him money when I will be in CdG. I'm speaking with my friend on Monday. I would ask him if our great-grandfather is at risk to be removed from his place. Send me a copy of your letter. I hope to fix everything. Have a nice weekend.

February 4, 2017
Celia to Salvatore:

Hi Salvatore, do you want me to send the money to you at the Via F... address or to you at your home? Here are the 2 letters to the cemetery (they are the same). Only one is specifically addressed to Maurizio Cassara.
Also, by the way, our great-grandfather is NOT listed in the cemetery records. I find this very strange.

Tell your friend he will have a big battle on his hands & the mayor's hands if they move him. I will pay the fee to keep him there. But I know you are a good negotiator & will hopefully fix this. You can claim my ignorance of Italian rules of the community. Have a good weekend.

June 25, 2016 and September 11, 2016
Signor Maurizio Cassara
Cimitero di Castellammare del Golfo
Via Euclide
91014 Castellammare del Golfo, Trapani, Sicily, Italy

Ciao Signor Cassara,

I met you this past May when my cousin Bernardo Como brought me to the cemetery to pay my respects to many family members. (Milano's, Vivona's, Galatioto's, Cartiera's, Giliberti's).

I had inquired into the location of my great-grandfather Lorenzo Milano who died 8 December 1939. The records did not show his location.

Fortunately, my cousin Maria Ciaravino Milano (widow of Lorenzo Milano who died 6 October 2010) showed me my great-grandfather's grave.

[When you leave the office building, take a right turn and walk to the end of the sidewalk (to the second closed gate). It is on that wall. I am including a photo.]

The engraving on the stone has faded so that it is very hard to read.

I am writing to inquire about the process and cost to clean and restore my great-grandfather's grave marker.

Your help in this matter will be greatly appreciated.

Molti saluti,

[I included the two previous photos from the chapter Locating the Grave of Great-Grandfather Lorenzo Milano]

February 17, 2017
Salvatore to Celia:

Hi Celia, how are you? I hope you are fine. Today I spoke with my friend in CdG and I was guaranteed about our grandfather's place. I will speak next Monday with Fontana to proceed with the work in tombstone. Next month, when I will go in CdG, I will choose the vase.
Sorry if I don't write you in these days but I'm very busy with my job. Now some moment of relax. I go to listen to some live music. Have a nice w. e.

February 17, 2017
Celia to Salvatore:

Hi Salvatore! We are doing well. How are you & your sons? I am so happy to hear that our binonno will stay in his grave. I will send the Euro out this week so you will have it in time to meet with Fontana. I will send it to you in care of your mom. Enjoy the music and have a wonderful weekend.

February 17, 2017
Salvatore to Celia:

I think it's better to send money to my office. Here is the address...

Celia A. Milano

February 28, 2017
Salvatore to Celia:

Hi Celia, I received your money a few minutes ago. I didn't understand the reason about 20 Euros plus. I'm going in CdG next Saturday (10 March). I hope to send you photos of tombstone. Kisses

February 28, 2017
Celia to Salvatore:

Hi Salvatore! I am happy you received the mail.
OK. About the 20 Euro. If I hire a company to do work, an employee will come to do the job. I pay by bank check to the company. If the employee (worker) does a good job, I will give that person a gratuity (tip) in cash in their hand (that the boss does not need to know about. Ha Ha, since you are a boss, you may not like to hear this!!!) The same as when you go for caffé normale & a cornetto. If it is considered inappropriate, then use it to buy some dolce for your mom.
I look forward to seeing the photos. Many many thanks!

March 12, 2017
Salvatore Messengered Celia on Facebook:

Tomorrow I'm going to choose the flowers case.

AMORE BONTÀ VIRTÙ
RIPULSERO NELLA VITA LABORIOSA
E CORRETTA DI MILANO LORENZO
DI ANNI 77 MORTO L' 8-12-1939
I FIGLI DOLENTI POSERO

March 12, 2017
Celia replied to Salvatore's Facebook Message:

Diomio!!! Fontana did a wonderful job!!!! Thank you!!!
Grazie!!!

March 13, 2017
Salvatore Messengered Celia on Facebook:

Which do you prefer? This one? or this one?

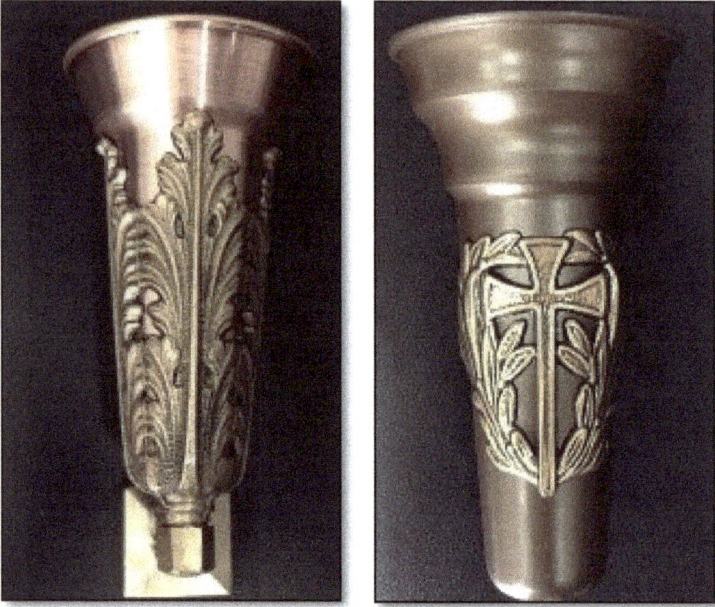

March 13, 2017
Celia Messengered Salvatore back on Facebook:

The 2nd one. It will look beautiful on the cleaned tombstone.
Thank you so much for doing this.

March 14, 2017

Salvatore Messengered Celia on Facebook:

March 14, 2017
Celia Messengered Salvatore back on Facebook:

OMG!! Dio mio!! Beautiful!!! I am crying, I am so happy!!
Grazie Salvatore
Salvatore...when I was at the cemetery, Maurizio Cassara
could not find the record for our great-grandfather. I do not
know why. Possibly from the war, as records could have
been destroyed. Do you know, if it is possible to obtain the
location or plot # of his grave??

March 14, 2017
Salvatore Messengered Celia back on Facebook:

I understand. Today I was with the boss of the cemetery, a friend of mine, and Maurizio. He knows all about our great-grandfather. You can take it easy our great-grandfather can rest quiet.

Celia to Salvatore:

Ok. Wonderful!! I am happy that Great-Grandfather Lorenzo can rest where he is. Thank you!! If it wasn't for you, this would not have been possible.

To Be Continued

Now that the gravestone of my great-grandfather Lorenzo Milano had been restored and there was no chance of him being removed from his grave, I continued my search for information regarding my other great-grandfather, Giuseppe Maria Vivona. As I mentioned before, I have written to and visited the Sicilian Comunes of Calatafimi, where he was born, and Castellammare del Golfo, where he raised his family. I also scoured the Statue of Liberty Ellis Island Foundation and Family Search websites. I found nothing about him. I was totally baffled by this. Yes, there were many passenger lists with the name Giuseppe Vivona, which I investigated, but none were him. I even wrote to the Vital Records Department for New York City, identified myself and included my credentials, but there was nothing. Oh, yes, he was listed as "father" on my Grandmother Rosaria Vivona's marriage record, but nowhere else. It was like he had vanished from the face of the earth.

Online, I belonged to a few genealogy research groups, including the Sicilian and Aeolian Islands group. Two of the members, knowing I had hit the proverbial "brick wall," mentioned the Antenati, an Italian Records website as another resource.
http://www.antenati.san.beniculturali.it

I figured; why not give it a try?

I logged on, typed in various combinations of dates, names and reviewed the results. Everything jived with what I had in my records. Then came the true test. I entered Giuseppe Vivona and Angela/Angelina Giliberti and then hit the search key while crossing my fingers.

Wooo Hooo!

I didn't find any records for Giuseppe, but I did find two new pieces of information.

The first record I found was the death record for Salvatore Vivona, their first-born child. A couple of years earlier, the Comune of Castellammare del Golfo, had sent me his birth record, but I always wondered why there had been no additional information for him. Salvatore was born in May of 1891, was a barber, and died in May of 1912 at the age of twenty-one. And of course, no cause of death was listed.

I couldn't imagine what my great-grandmother Angela had gone through coping with his death. I did know that she immigrated to the U.S. the following year and arrived at Ellis Island in September of 1913, with two of her young children.

No clue where her husband, Giuseppe Maria, was in all of this.

The second record I found was for Antonino Vivona, another son whom I did not know about. The record states that he was a barber and died in October of 1918 at the age of fifteen.

Dio mio! My God! So young.

I wrote to the Comune in Castellammare del Golfo requesting his birth and death records and soon after received a reply from Signora

Rosa Giabino that included both. Antonino was born in October of 1903. His death certificate only listed the date of death but no cause.

So how did a fifteen-year-old boy die?

I referred back to the letter written by Elisabetta Vivona Olivet, my grandmother, Rosario's sister. In it, she states that both Antonino and Salvatore died from the Spanish flu, but I question this, as the "Spanish flu" outbreak did not occur in Europe until 1918. According to my research, which was mindboggling, the flu outbreak occurred in the U.S. much earlier, was ignored by the U.S. government and the flu spread to Europe with our troop movements during World War I. So, I believe that Antonino, who died in October 1918, was possibly a victim of the flu.

http://virus.stanford.edu/uda/

https://en.wikipedia.org/wiki/1918_flu_pandemic#Hypotheses_about_source

After doing further research, I realized that Salvatore's death may have been caused naturally, by accident, by an outbreak of cholera.

http://www.lodico.org/mike/images/Notes/Giuseppe-Angelina-Lodico.html

http://www.nejm.org/doi/full/10.1056/NEJM191109281651315

...or, by the heat wave of 1911 in Italy and Spain that had devastating consequences by creating diseases via microorganisms in fish, plants and man. https://www.cairn.info/revue-annales-de-demographie-historique-2010-2-page-147.htm

Another mystery.

As for their father, my elusive great-grandfather, on August 16, 2014 during a conversation I had with my cousin, Betty Olivet Palumbo, she stated that her mother, Elisabetta, told her that Giuseppe Maria Vivona died of double lumbar pneumonia at age forty-five. So, I am assuming Giuseppe Maria Vivona died in 1910. The death date is unknown as the Comune does not have his death record. And so, the mystery continues. There are still "black holes" of missing data, but, hopefully I will have more answers before I finally leave this earth.

P.S. – A Request

I started thinking again, which was not a good thing for those on the receiving end. As I mentioned before, the Cimitero Comunale did not have a record of my great-grandfather Lorenzo Milano being buried there. Plus, now I had two more great-uncles who died and I didn't know where they were buried, if anywhere. I didn't know how the bodies of those dying in the flu pandemic were handled. I wondered how many people were buried in the cemetery but never listed in the registry books.

I contacted my friend Enzo and my cousins Salvatore and Felice for an opinion of an idea.

Hello Salvatore, Enzo and Felice,

Every day I thank God for Cousin Maria who showed Bernardo and me the grave of our great-grandfather, as the cemetery had NO record of him being buried there. So, I started to do some research into cemeteries in CdelG.

There are websites such as Find A Grave that allows one to search for death information and photos of gravestones. In fact, I belong to a genealogy society that has photographed all the gravestones in our county here in Vero Beach (https://irgs.org/cemeteryRecords.php)

I have searched the internet and I do not find any for Castellammare del Golfo. So, now again I am seeking advice. I am wondering if the town of CdelG would allow me to begin a project of photographing all the gravestones. In addition, I would need from the cemetery a map of the land and the plots. Do you think this is possible??

Enzo composed the first letter and emailed it to me. I signed and sent it back so he could hand deliver it to the Mayor's office in October. There was no reply as the Mayor was on vacation, in Brooklyn, NY, of all places, for the Columbus Day celebration at the Castellammaresi Club.

I decided that the Mayor needed to understand why I was requesting this project, so I composed another letter and included my family tree chart.

Celia A. Milano

The Mayor of Castellammare del Golfo
Corso Bernardo Mattarella, 24
91014 Castellammare del Golfo, Trapani, Italy
19 November 2017

Dear Mr. Coppola,

My name is Celia Milano. I am 65 years of age, born in New York City, raised in Yonkers New York and I am the family genealogist. I am the great-granddaughter of Lorenzo Milano and Anna Galatioto, and Giuseppe Maria Vivona and Angelina Giliberti who lived and raised their families in Castellammare del Golfo. Please see the attached chart.

Recently my friend Enzo Filogamo was very kind and delivered a letter to your office for me. You must be wondering, "Why is this woman requesting permission to see the land plans for the cemetery and to photograph the graves?"

It is a tribute to those people who have lived, worked, raised families, and died in your town. In addition, it will be a family history record for those, like myself, seeking any information regarding their ancestors.

In May 2016, I visited with my cousin Maria Ciaravino Milano and met more new cousins. During this time, I went to the Cimiterio Comunale to visit the grave of my great-grandfather Lorenzo Milano and other relatives. I took photos of some of the graves and they now reside on the website, Find-A-Grave. http://bit.ly/2QEzdbc

In addition, to documenting cemetery stones, my hope is also to photograph the postings of notification of exhumation.

I thank you in advance for your consideration of this project.

Sincerely, Celia Milano

I received a positive response to my two requests to the Mayor's office for my project to photograph the gravestones in the Cimitero Comunale on Via Euclid!!

Comune di Castellammare del Golfo
Libero Consorzio Comunale di Trapani
Settore III° - Infrastrutture

Prot. N 6669 del 0 8 FEB. 2018

alla Sig.ra **Celia Milano**

USA

Oggetto: Autorizzazione a fotografare le lapidi dei loculi esistenti all'interno del Cimitero Comunale di Castellammare del Golfo.

In riferimento alla Vostra nota n. 47405 del 19.10.2017, si comunica che la S.V. è stata autorizzata dal Sindaco protempore, a fotografare le lapidi dei propri defunti sepolti nel Cimitero Comunale di Castellammare del Golfo.

Si allega copia della nota n. 47405 del 19.10.2017 con autorizzazione firmata dal Sindaco.

Il Tecnico Comunale
(Geom. G. Giangiunto)

Il Responsabile del III Settore
(Ing. Simone Culmano)

Translation:

Subject: Authorization to photograph the tombstones of the existing niches inside the Municipal Cemetery of Castellammare del Golfo.

In reference to your note n. 47405 of 19.10.2017, we note that the S.V. and was authorized by the Mayor pro-tempore, to photograph the tombstones of their dead buried in the Cemetery Comunale of Castellammare del Golfo.

∞∞∞∞

I booked my Alitalia airline ticket and Cousin Felice offered to provide transportation from the airport and prepare my room at Bed and Breakfast Nonna Giò. I texted Salvatore and Enzo my travel plans. All was set for the trip to Castellammare del Golfo in May of 2018.

When word spread throughout the community of my friends, neighbors, family, in-laws and out-laws that I was headed back to Sicily, most of them asked, if during this visit, I could keep a daily diary detailing all my experiences. In reply, I mentioned that some days, especially the morning rituals would be mundane and no one would be interested in hearing about them. The responses varied but in essence, I was told, "You've got to be kidding, right? You'll be in Sicily. Did you hear me, Sicily? How can it be boring?"

So, instead of bringing my little tablet, I bought a Samsung Chromebook to write a journal. In addition, after speaking with my brother Roy, the computer whiz, he suggested that I upload my photographs periodically, just in case the camera got zapped at the airport when I flew back home.

So the journal began...

The Journal

On My Way Back to Sicily

WEDNESDAY, MAY 2, 2018

I'm excited to be going back to Castellammare del Golfo! Unbelievable that it's been two years since I was there.

Vito and I left the house early, gassed up the car, and were on I-95 heading to Miami by 10:45 a.m. The weather was great, no rain this time. Traffic wasn't too bad until the West Palm Beach (PBI), Ft. Lauderdale (FLL) and Miami (MIA) airport exits.

Vito can't do the six-hour round-trip drive, so he stayed overnight in Miami. We arrived at the Embassy Suites, checked in by 1:30 p.m., and at 4:30 p.m., we took the hotel jitney to the airport. On the jitney, we met a young couple from Argentina who had backpacked around Florida and the States.

We arrived at the Alitalia Departure area where Vito helped me check-in my baggage. We hugged and kissed goodbye and off I went to Concourse H. As I was sitting in the departure gate waiting area, I met Tom and Myra from Palm Beach who had just sold their house to a construction firm after hurricane Irma issues. They're going to Italy, the Bari area for four weeks, then to Albania for a month.

I also saw a gentleman who had a familiar face. I went over to him, introduced myself and asked him if he had been to Yugoslavia in June 1989. He said many people approach him and guessed he had that kind of face. But in answer to my question, yes, he was in Yugoslavia at that time. I mentioned the cities I visited with a group of friends and he nodded his head. He was one of the local people who helped tourists, quietly without the government knowing. Two things I remembered. First, staying in Dubrovnik and receiving a small business-sized card with the address of the home. If we were stopped by anyone, we were to say that we were Americans visiting relatives for the first time. Second, being in the town of Mostar and hearing gunshots. Unknown to us, the revolution was beginning. When I think back on it, I shudder. A little too unreal for me. I later learned that the Mostar Bridge – which I'd stood on – was bombed and demolished.

Time to board!

I was in seat 25C. The man next to me was already asleep and slept most of the trip. My vegan meal was served at 9:00 p.m. before anyone else's. During dinner, my seatmate told me that it was his first time traveling to Italy and he was going to tour Rome, Florence, and Tuscany.

After dinner, I watched BBC News. When that was over, I noticed that the lights were out and everyone was settling in. I was lucky and slept maybe three hours. Lots of snoring, two babies crying, and the little girl across from me was bruxing (grinding) her teeth all night.

Poor thing!

The plane arrived in Rome at 11:55 a.m., Thursday morning. We weren't in the main terminal, so I had to run with the group to take the train to the main terminal and had to hurry through the airport to customs control. I was panicking when a young man said to me to go to the front of the line as everyone who has a close connecting flight does. He didn't have to do it this time. I felt weird doing it, but I did. The customs man was very nice. I told him I had a connecting flight in forty-five minutes and was nervosa (nervous) that I would miss it. He smiled and said not to worry, as he stamped my passport and checked me in. Then, I was off and running to find gate B14, which was very far through the domestic terminal.

Deja vu!

I got to the gate, sweating and by the skin of my teeth again. This time there was a bus filled with passengers and we were driven to the far side of the airport, which I could swear I just came from. The plane was a small one, thirty rows of six seats, three on each side. But to board, I had to carry myself, backpack and small rolling suitcase up the stairs to seat 8C. My back and legs were shaking.

Unbelievable!

Instead of taking off at 1:20 p.m., which I busted my butt to make, the plane took off at 1:50 p.m. and landed in Palermo an hour later. FYI: Passengers whose flights originated outside of Italy had to pick up their luggage at the carousel, bring it to another area where the bags go through another TSA scan and you present your passport.

Nino, a colleague of Cousin Felice greeted me when I exited the airport. He drove me the fifty minutes to Bed and Breakfast Nonna Giò in Castellammare del Golfo where Felice was waiting. We hugged and kissed. Felice brought my luggage up to my room on the second floor, the same one I stayed in last time. As we chatted, and added Felice to WhatsApp, he apologized for not being at the airport as he had been in Palermo visiting his father in the hospital. He had a stent placed in his carotid artery.

OMG!

Felice said he was doing well and would be released soon. After Felice left, I began settling in and took a shower, which felt great after twenty plus hours. Exhausted, I dropped onto the bed at 7:30 p.m.

FRIDAY, MAY 4, 2018

Yikes! I slept almost twelve hours.

I couldn't believe it was almost 9:00 a.m. As I opened the balcony door, the air felt cool and it was raining. I was glad I brought my LL Bean rain slicker, although no umbrella. I had it in my hand when I was packing but didn't think I would need it, so put it aside.

Oh well, it doesn't matter.

All I could think about was walking the streets and caffé normale. For those of you who know me, it is pointless to say that I needed coffee. I got ready and left ASAP. I walked and soaked up the sights and sounds that I'd missed so much.

You know where I was headed, right? Cafe Garibaldi!

There were no tables outside that day due to the rain, so I walked through the shop to the back where I saw Vito Alfano, the owner. We exchanged many hugs and kisses and then as if by magic, the caffé normale, a stuffed spinach cornetto and a glass of water appeared.

I told Vito, "To die for. I waited two years to taste this again." He laughed as he asked about my husband, Vito, and how my family research was progressing. He then introduced me to his beautiful wife, Elisabetta, a lovely young woman. While we were talking, I learned that Vito had many family members in Texas, Wisconsin and Ohio. He and Elisabetta went to New York City for their honeymoon but didn't know at the time that they had relatives in the States. They both said that when they returned, they were contacted by the family in Texas. Each family has since visited each other. Vito is still in awe of the experience and said he now fully understands my research.

I needed to walk again, so after a while, I left to go to the fruit and vegetable stand on the opposite end of Corso Garibaldi to buy fruit, specifically strawberries. FYI: The grapefruits and lemons are as big as your head. On the way back, I saw a store, Sottosopra that displayed umbrellas and purchased one for €6 and stashed it in my backpack.

I continued on and went to the Gastronomia L'Angelo Del Buongustaio deli on the corner of Corso Garibaldi and Corso Bernardo Mattarella, where I said, "Ciao," to the owners, Signor and Signora Fontana. I noticed some cartolinas (postcards) pinned on the wall and spotted the one I'd sent them two years earlier. I pointed to it and said, "Io (me)."

They said in unison, "Ah, Vero Beach."

Their sandwiches were so good that I ordered one of pesto, olives, cheese, and prosciutto to munch on later.

As I was walking, I saw Felice and he said, "This afternoon at 16:00, I am taking you to visit Zia Maria at the assisted living house. It is very difficult to find, and I want to take you there the first time." It was very sweet of him as he was very busy with the store and his transportation business.

Note to myself: I need to put the photo I brought with me into my backpack.

What a ride to visit Maria. Wow!

There was no way in hell I would've found it on my own. We saw Maria, hugged, kissed and visited with her for a little while. Her health was failing and my heart went out to her. I gave her the photo of her, my cousin Lorenzo (her husband) and me at Scopello, which my sister Laurie took of us in 1999. She hadn't seen me in two years but made the connection.

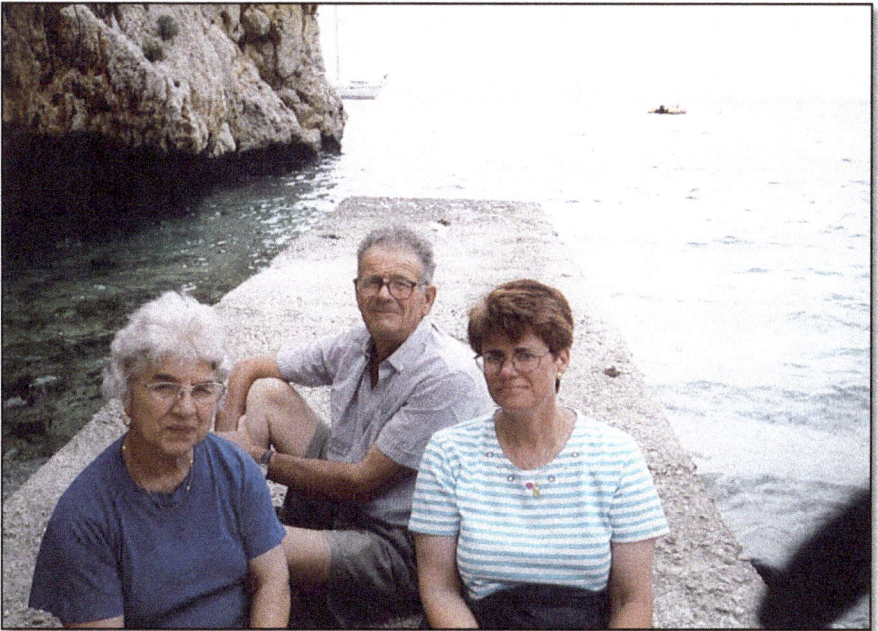

Felice drove us back to the store where we continued our catch-up conversation and, yes, we had to use Google translate to help with some fuzzy areas.

SATURDAY, MAY 5, 2018

It was chilly the next morning as I walked to Cafe Garibaldi. Vito and I said, "Ciao, buongiorno. (Hello, good morning.)" He told me his mom made a cake with apples that morning.

OMG!

Mrs. Alfano's cakes are absolutely delicious, so I ordered a slice with my caffé normale. He asked what my plans were that day and I told him I was going to the cemetery. He knew of my request to the town about photographing the gravestones and then to upload them to the Find-A-Grave website for other researchers to use. Plus, I was hoping to find my other binonno (great-grandfather) Giuseppe Maria Vivona and his two sons, Salvatore and Antonino.

I asked Vito the best route to walk, and he marked the map for me. It was about a mile or 1.7 km one way. He said that there was an open market on Saturday, so it would be crowded. I thanked him and then left for my walk to the cemetery. I noted some shops that I wanted to browse in during my time there – and a bakery, Pasticceria 2000.

I arrived at the outskirts of the market, which reminded me of the large Englishtown Auction in New Jersey. The market had anything you could want, from household items to clothing, shoes, skateboards, fishing rods, books, etc. I stopped at the florist and purchased flowers for my great-grandfather, Lorenzo Milano. As I walked into the cemetery, I couldn't believe my eyes. There was my friend Enzo walking down the street.

I said, "Ciao Enzo. It's Celia."

He said, "Oh my, I thought you were not coming until a little later in the month, but this morning I thought I saw you walking to Vito's."

Many hugs and kisses later, he introduced me to his friend, Leonardo. They asked what I was doing there and I said I was looking for "Mio binonno, my great-grandfather, Lorenzo Milano." So, they walked with me as I looked and after a while they continued on to their relatives' graves. When I found the grave, I grabbed the tall ladder, maneuvered it to where I could reach the stone, climbed up three steps to take the wilting flowers out of the vase, climbed down, got water, climbed back up, filled the vase, added my flowers and back down the ladder again.

I did the same thing for his son, my great-uncle, Lorenzo Milano. I then walked around the cemetery taking photos. I decided during this time that the most important part of my cemetery project should be to photograph the gravestones that show signs of wear and don't have flowers on them. I also saw some postings on mausoleum houses and graves that I believe were notices of exhumation.

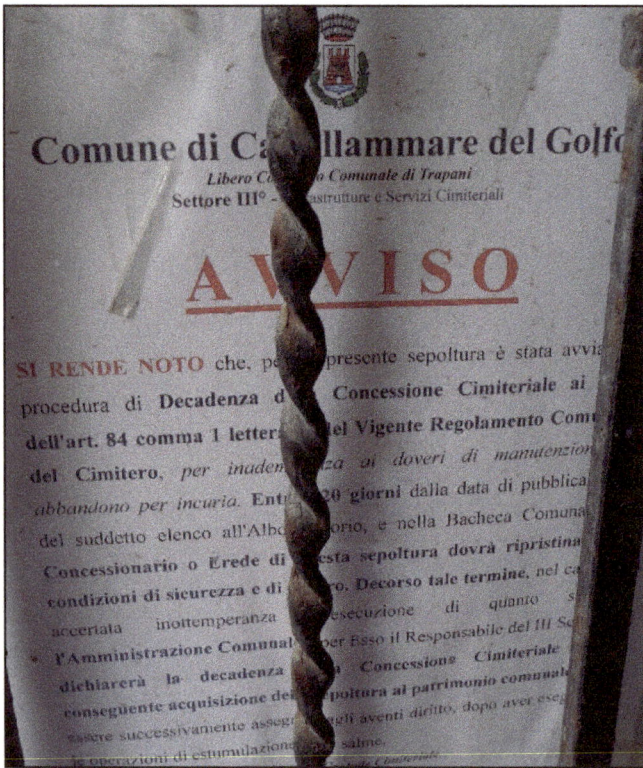

I'll ask Felice or wait until I get back to the B&B to translate them.

I stayed for a few hours and it was warm walking back, so I stopped for a small gelato and water at Cafe Garibaldi, where I saw Elisabetta and we talked awhile. She was from northern Italy but her father was Sicilian and came from a nearby town. Then on to the B&B where I saw Felice and his parents. I was so happy as his father had been in the hospital the day I arrived. They both looked well. We chatted awhile. And yes, the notice at the cemetery was for exhumation.

It was late afternoon and time to upload the photos, charge the camera and write. As I stated, I thought it would be advantageous if I kept a daily electronic journal of my trip, so I wouldn't have to rely on my memory for all the details.

After a couple of hours, my stomach decided that it was time to have something to eat. So, I walked to the Corso Garibaldi and decided to have dinner at Trattoria La Maidda, which Felice had recommended. The restaurant was at the pedestrian-only intersection of Corso Garibaldi and Corso Bernardo Mattarella. It was a nice place with seating both outside and inside. I chose inside, as it was getting breezy. The waiter, Roberto, was very cordial and described some of the dishes to me. I decided to have aqua fizzante, a glass of white wine and a large salad with grilled mushrooms and zucchini. When the salad arrived, the mushroom cap was huge and sliced. The dinner was wonderful, as was the service.

A walk was definitely needed, so I continued on Corso Garibaldi, which becomes Via Giacomo Puccini, and decided to stop in to see Leonardo and Cristina who owned the Sikelia Sicilian Souvenir shop. Cristina was there and we caught up on news. She and Leo had married last November.

Leo was working part-time at the new hotel that just opened a year ago, Hotel Sopra Le Mura. So, he was hopping back and forth between both places. Cristina was going to Spain the following week as her father was having surgery, but her friend would run the shop with Leo. She mentioned the time that my friend Eszter Vajda (You, Me & Sicily) had come to film their shop and couldn't thank me enough.

Cristina also mentioned that there was a documentary film of old Castellammare del Golfo, which she thinks I would enjoy seeing. She said she would send the link. We said, "A presto. (See you soon.)," and I continued on my walk to the Villa Comunale.

Celia A. Milano

SUNDAY, MAY 6, 2018

I was up early to meet Enzo at the Café Garibaldi at 9:00 a.m. The place was busy when I arrived. I went inside said, "Buongiorno" to Vito, ordered a cappuccino and looked to see what his mom had baked that morning; a crusty closed pocket of warm sweet ricotta, similar to what's in a cannoli.

To Die For. Scrumptious!

It was a beautiful morning, so I decided to sit outside. When Vito brought out my order, he had a few minutes to talk. As he had expressed an interest in my family chart, I brought it with me, just in case. He was shaking his head when I started to unfold it, as it was five feet wide, but he liked the layout and perused it. He knew several people, which freaked me out.

During this time, Enzo and his friend, Leonardo, arrived. Enzo ordered the same as me and Leonardo had a caffé normale. Enzo looked at the chart and also pointed to several people he knew. I only thought he knew Cousin Bernardo, but I was surprised to learn that he also knew Cousin Lorenzo. Ironically, he told me that many years ago he and Lorenzo were having coffee and talking when Lorenzo told him he had to leave early because he had to meet cousins coming from America.

I said, "Dio mio! That was my sister and me in 1999."

He said "Yes."

We laughed.

Way too coincidental for me, no?

We talked about our health, family, the cemetery photos and the many new businesses in Castellammare, as both Corsos, Garibaldi and Bernardo Mattarella have expanded.

Before we parted, Enzo asked, "What do you want to see Erice, Marsala, Segesta, Selinunte?" He offered to drive me around to see some different places.

"You tell me where, when, and the time" I said. How very sweet and generous.

Before I forget: I stopped at the Bancomat near the cafe and had no problem using the Charles Schwab debit card. Wooo-Hooo!

∞∞∞∞

Now that I had some fuel in me, it was time to walk the mile to the cemetery. I had two missions. The first was to find the graves of my two great-uncles, Antonino and Salvatore, and their father, my great-grandfather Giuseppe Maria Vivona. The second was to photograph the gravestones in the cemetery.

Why?

As I mentioned previously, it was a genealogy project for the people of the town.

I stopped at the florist tent outside the cemetery and bought two bouquets of flowers to place on the graves of both Lorenzo Milanos, my great-grandfather and great-uncle. As I walked around taking photos, my earlier decision was confirmed. The graves that were recent and/or had flowers, I would not photograph, as they were being kept up. It was the ones that looked abandoned, and, as such, might be exhumed, that I cared about most.

Close to noon, I decided to go to the office and ask about the location of Mrs. Sanfilippo's grave. As I mentioned earlier, I met "Mama" two years ago and had a little adventure. The manager was there with four younger men who were talking. When I asked for help many languages – except English – were used.

Oh boy.

Slowly I explained that Mrs. Sanfilippo had died the prior summer. When asked her maiden name, and I said, "No conosco. (I do not know.)" Based on the death date, it was determined that her maiden name was Bussa, the grave location was noted, the manager closed the office and we were on our way to her grave. We walked to the far side of that section of the cemetery, arrived at an open mausoleum area and took the elevator to the third floor. The manager showed me the grave, and I thanked him before he left. I placed flowers in the vase and took a photo for her granddaughters, Nina and

Danielle. I would never have known it was Mama Sanfilippo, as her married name was not on the stone and the photo was one from many years ago, but as I looked closer and saw the mischief in her eyes, I said to myself, "Yes, that's Mama." As I walked back to the elevator, I looked at the spectacular view. Rest easy, Mama.

I spent a little more time walking around taking photos then decided it was time to leave. On the way back to Via Sole, I stopped at the pharmacy, which was a very interesting store. You just didn't walk in, you had to enter through a gate, where you were greeted and asked to browse around. If you needed help, they were right there to assist you. I found what I needed, went to the checkout counter, out through the exit gate and was on my way. As I arrived at the B&B, I saw Felice's father, who looked great, and my cousin Elena. After more hugs and kisses, we chatted for a while to catch up.

∞∞∞∞

Later that afternoon, I was hungry and decided to have dinner. I went back to the Trattoria La Maidda and was happy I did. I kept it simple - pane, aqua frizzante, homemade fresh spaghetti in pomodoro sauce with grilled eggplant and topped with fresh cheese. The spaghetti was hand-made and fresh like Cousin Maria made. To Die For!

To complete my dinner, I had a caffé normale. After thanking Roberto and Gaspare, I was on my way. I turned the corner and headed toward Vernaci's and Villa Comunale. After one scoop of pistachio gelato, and watching the outstanding view of the marina, I continued my walk down to Piazza Petrolo.

OMG!

Something was going on at the Hotel Al Madarig, as there were many people and cars. The Sunday passaggiata (stroll) was in full swing and Piazza Petrolo was packed. Yes, that area has also grown with more restaurants, although the huge crowd couldn't have been the norm.

While I was walking in the piazza and taking photos, I saw a young father taking a photo of his wife and baby. I approached them and asked if they wanted a photo of the three of them. He showed me the camera on his phone, and I took some photos for them. I said it was very important for their family history. They thanked me.

It was getting late and I was tired, so I started walking back to the B&B. Plus, the more I thought about my conversation with Enzo, the more I thought about seeing the Marsala Salt Pans, so I texted Enzo.

"Good," he said. "We will discuss it over coffee tomorrow morning around 9:00 a.m. at Vito's."

MONDAY, MAY 7, 2018

When I arrived at the café, Enzo was already sitting outside, waiting for his caffé normale and cake. We said, "Ciao. Boungiorno." When I went in to see Vito to order my cappuccino, I looked to see what his mom had made that morning: a thin ricotta cheesecake laced with chocolate encased in a very thick biscuit.

OMG!

I also told Vito that I would pay for Enzo, as he had snuck in and paid for mine the day before.

When I sat down at the table, Enzo said that we would be driving to Marsala, as it was a beautiful morning with no rain nor clouds and should only take one hour. Over breakfast, we continued our discussion of the good and bad points of technology. As we looked around, we saw both the very young and the very old checking their phones and tablets. We both laughed as we had Information Technology in common specifically, programming and computers. I told Enzo that I was becoming "vecchia (old)" as the technology changed every day and it was too much to keep up. I told him that my husband, Vito, who was a "tech dinosaur," knew more than me. He laughed, as he was eleven years older than me. After that comment, Enzo opened both his phone and tablet to get GPS directions for Marsala, more tech in addition to the English and Italian word jumble. We both laughed hysterically. When we finished breakfast, he started getting up but I told him to sit down for a few minutes and I went inside to pay our bills.

When I returned, Enzo said, "Andiamo."

We walked up to the other side of Corso Garibaldi to get his car and off we went. At the gas station, I wanted to pay but both he and the young attendant laughed and ignored my waving credit card. Enzo drove us along some back roads (SS187) where the scenery was absolutely breathtaking. There was no way I could've taken photos, but it was etched into my memory. Olive groves, vineyards, sheep, windmills for energy, some solar farms, and country houses with solar panels on the roofs, which all tied back to our continuing tech conversation.

Along the way, we passed a town that was very small, Enzo said maybe one thousand people lived there. It looked like a few streets with a small-town center.

Gorgeous. Mmmmm...I wonder if there is a small apartment for rent.

We arrived at the Mothia Salt Pans, parked, and found our way to the entrance walkway to see the men working out in several different pans. The pans were interconnected and the salt content increased as the water flowed along. It was a fascinating process about which most people have no concept. We also went into the museum where photos displayed the whole process.

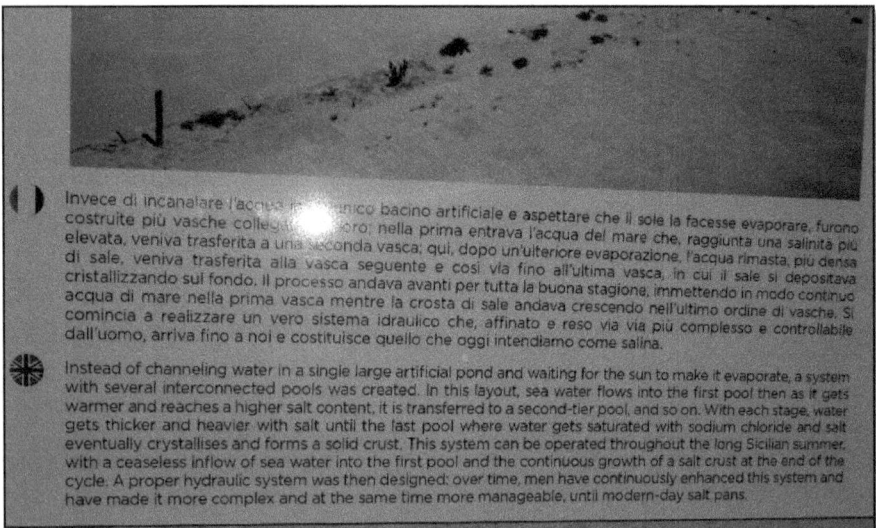

Invece di incanalare l'acqua in un unico bacino artificiale e aspettare che il sole la facesse evaporare, furono costruite più vasche collegate tra loro; nella prima entrava l'acqua del mare che, raggiunta una salinità più elevata, veniva trasferita a una seconda vasca; qui, dopo un'ulteriore evaporazione, l'acqua rimasta, più densa di sale, veniva trasferita alla vasca seguente e così via fino all'ultima vasca, in cui il sale si depositava cristallizzando sul fondo. Il processo andava avanti per tutta la buona stagione, immettendo in modo continuo acqua di mare nella prima vasca mentre la crosta di sale andava crescendo nell'ultimo ordine di vasche. Si comincia a realizzare un vero sistema idraulico che, affinato e reso via via più complesso e controllabile dall'uomo, arriva fino a noi e costituisce quello che oggi intendiamo come salina.

Instead of channeling water in a single large artificial pond and waiting for the sun to make it evaporate, a system with several interconnected pools was created. In this layout, sea water flows into the first pool then as it gets warmer and reaches a higher salt content, it is transferred to a second-tier pool, and so on. With each stage, water gets thicker and heavier with salt until the last pool where water gets saturated with sodium chloride and salt eventually crystallises and forms a solid crust. This system can be operated throughout the long Sicilian summer, with a ceaseless inflow of sea water into the first pool and the continuous growth of a salt crust at the end of the cycle. A proper hydraulic system was then designed: over time, men have continuously enhanced this system and have made it more complex and at the same time more manageable, until modern-day salt pans.

We stayed for a few hours and then headed back to Castellammare del Golfo via the autostrada. Then Enzo veered off onto more back roads with more small towns, farms and isolated country homes. It was absolutely breathtakingly, clean and so very green. At one point, we were almost as high as the town of Erice.

I said, "Maria Grammatico Pasticceria has the best marzipan."

He said, "You know this place?"

I told him, "In 1999 my sister Laurie, myself, Cousin Lorenzene (yes, another Cousin Lorenzo) and his wife Francesca went there. It's a great town, but the walk up the mountain would make my walking to and from the cemetery everyday look like nothing."

He laughed.

Enzo dropped me off at the B&B, I thanked him, and we said, "Ciao!"

Felice asked where I'd been all day, so I explained that Enzo had surprised me and taken me to Marsala. Felice just shook his head and laughed. I asked him about Piazza Petrolo and all the cars and people there the prior night. He said that two candidates running for mayor had events, one at Hotel Al Madarig and the other at the Comune arena on Corso Bernardo Mattarelle. That explained it.

It was time to eat, so I went back up to the Corso Garibaldi to Timpesti e Carmarii for a sandwich of sheep's cheese, ham, lettuce, olive oil, and lemon. The bread was scrumptious, like I used to have in New York and New Jersey. And thick, too, so much so, I had to eat it with a fork. Some people stopped by my table to say hello, introduce themselves and peruse my family history chart. Word had spread again about my family's origins in the town.

After my late lunch, I continued walking to the Piazza Petrolo, where I saw a man scuba diving around the rocks in the sea.

Then I saw a couple trying to take a selfie, so I asked if I could take the photo for them. They asked where I was from and how I found my way to their town. I gave them the short version of how my great-grandparents lived there and raised their children, three of whom went to America. I explained that I was there to walk the streets my great-grandparents had walked and document my family history. They saw my camera and asked to take a photo of me with the sea in the background. They were a very sweet couple.

I continued walking around some small streets, passed by the Madrice church, back up the Corsos Garibaldi and Bernardo Mattarelle to the Villa Comunale to take in the cool breeze and the view of the marina from above.

Gorgeous! Too bad I can't pitch a tent here for three weeks and see this killer view every morning.

TUESDAY, MAY 8, 2018

After greeting another beautiful morning, I was soon on the way to my favorite café. Vito greeted me, and I ordered a cappuccino, accompanied by a crusty pocket of cream and lemon/lime filling topped by another fabulous crust with a sprinkling of confectioners' sugar. Mama Alfano was a wonderful baker.

As I was people-watching, Enzo's friend, Leonardo, stopped by. We were able to understand each other's conversation of mixed Italian and English. He asked if I wanted to walk with him that morning.

I said, "Yes!"

We strolled down the Corso Garibaldi, which becomes Via Giacomo Puccini, then made a right-hand turn onto the Piazza Petrolo, continued to the Castle and down the stairs to see what the fishermen had caught that morning.

After sauntering around, we continued to Cala Marina, up the steep hills to Corso Bernardo Mattarelle, which was near Vernaci's, the Comune building and the Villa Comunale. As always, I took some photos along the way. We continued our stroll down the Corso to the main pedestrian intersection where we said, "Ciao."

I had some errands to run. I went to the Post Office to buy francobolli (stamps) for postcards, and then stopped by the "Mercato Frutta e Verdura," the fruit and vegetable vendor near Piazza Petrolo. There I bought fresh soaked olives in oil from a barrel and some strawberries for snacking.

When I arrived back at the B&B, Felice and I discussed The Sicilian Project. It's a non-profit organization, which provides free English lessons to schoolchildren in a camp setting. He knew that I was on the board of directors and wanted to host a camp in town. He suggested that I speak with the school superintendent, Professore Salvatore Tinnirello. Felice marked the building for me on my map.

Another goal for me to achieve!

Afterwards, I went to dinner at 2:30 p.m. at Trattoria La Maidda. I ordered fried calamari, a small (not very) green salad, aqua frizzante, and then topped off with caffé normale. Delicious!

I needed to stretch after that fabulous meal, so I walked towards the Castle. As I passed the new hotel, Sopra Le Mura, I looked inside and saw Leo Gallo, who also owns Sikelia Sicilian Souvenirs. I went inside and he was happy to see me, as Cristina told him I was in town.

He looked very well and kept busy working in both places. About then, some people came in looking for a room with breakfast. After they signed in, I asked Leo how many rooms were in the hotel and he said thirteen at the time, but that they are adding two or three more across the way. The town, especially during their tourist season of May through September, was definitely growing. We talked a little more and then said, "A presto. (See you soon)."

Around 7:00 p.m., I had a yen for something sweet to eat so I walked to Vito's shop and had a gelato of dark chocolate with chunks of hard chocolate and vanilla with pineapple. Wow!

Two of the other shop owners came in to say "Ciao" to Vito and have gelatos. They also came over to see my chart, as everyone knew by then that I carried it in my backpack, which was always with me.

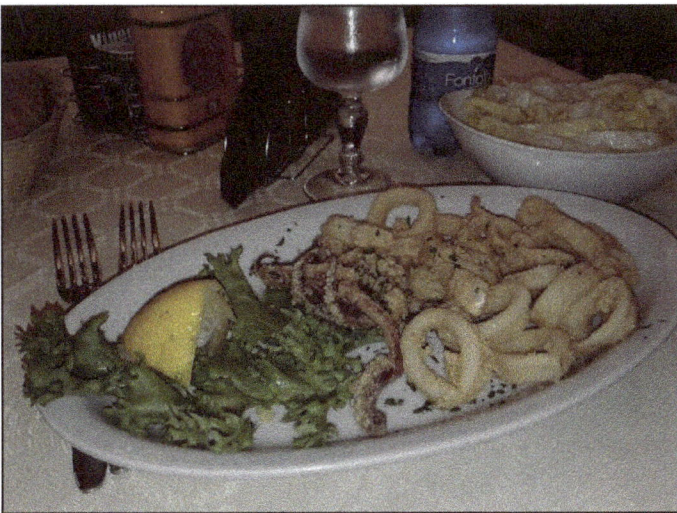

WEDNESDAY, MAY 9, 2018

I was up and out early. Since Vito's Café Garibaldi was closed, I decided to try Tipicamente. As I rounded the corner onto the Corso Garibaldi, I saw Enzo.

He said, "Vito is closed."

"Yes, I know," I said. "Let's try Tipicamente."

We sat outside and ordered two cappuccinos, a sfogliatella for me and a small breakfast sandwich for Enzo. During our conversation, Enzo said he was going to drive me to the spiaggia (the beach) after breakfast. I insisted on paying and off we went to get Enzo's car, a small boxy Fiat, which was parked on the other side of the Corso Garibaldi.

We drove to the beach where there were more new restaurants and, surprisingly, amusement rides for the kids that weren't there two years ago. I asked Enzo about all the new shops and stores and how they all survived together. He said the tourists came May through September and sometimes October, depending on the weather. The remainder of the year the stores were either closed or had modified hours.

Similar to our Jersey shore, no?

Enzo said that Vito Alfano and his wife Elisabetta sometimes went to Orlando in Florida.

I said, "Orlando is only an hour or so from me with 'la macchina.' (a car.)"

He couldn't believe it. "Really? I can fly from Brooklyn near my brother to Orlando in two hours, see the mouse and you?"

I nodded my head and laughed.

After the beach, Enzo took me to the mountain town of Alcamo, where many Castellammaresi had summer homes. The town was jammed with people and cars.

My God!

He told me there are about 500,000 people in Alcamo and approximately 16,000 in Castellammare del Golfo. He gave me the fifty-cent tour, and then said, "I will show you our summer house." It was a large beautiful two-story house, with two separate living areas for the family, a garage, garden, and, of course, the famous olive grove. It was also near the train station. After touring other homes, we headed back to Castellammare del Golfo.

I thanked him for the outing and said, "A presto."

It was still early enough, so I walked up to the school in which the director, Professore Salvatore Tinnirello had his office. At the reception desk, I asked if I could see him for five minutes. The woman checked, and I was asked into his office. I thanked him for seeing me and began telling him about The Sicilian Project - the free English camps for children that we sponsor - and asked if he was interested. He said, "Yes." I mentioned that the board president, Alfred Zappala, lived in Catania and would contact him. He asked where I was from and why I was in Castellammare del Golfo. I told him my parenti came from there and I came to visit cousins and friends. He gave me his email and personal cell phone number. I thanked him and continued my walk.

I stopped at the B&B to email the news to Alfred and then went out and about again. I explored a different route through new streets, took photos, talked to people along the way, and then found myself near the Piazza Petrolo. Okay, another route to walk.

During my stroll, I met a young woman from California whose husband had come to do his family research.

See, I'm not the only one.

I walked along until I arrived at La Timpa, an outdoor restaurant overlooking the water. It was time for a nosh. I ordered a tuna, ham, tomato, mozzarella, corn and olive salad.

OMG!

And the pane (bread) was the color of daffodils. I'm not usually a bread eater, but with a little olive oil, it was yummy.

THURSDAY, MAY 10, 2018

I was still in awe that I was in that town. As I meandered that morning, my feet took me to the Café, where I ordered caffé normale and a breakfast pocket filled with prosciutto, tomato, and cheese. Enzo stopped by to talk and then we walked awhile. We both had errands to run, so we said, "A presto."

You know where I headed then, right?

As I continued up Corso Garibaldi towards the cemetery, I heard someone call my name. It was Mr. Buccaletto, Felice's father, at the Roxy Bar chatting with his friends. Hugs, kisses, and introductions followed. It was so good to see him. Note: The majority of the "bars" were open early in the morning for caffé normale and for people to gather and talk.

Usually the drivers were very courteous during my walks up the Corso to Via Giglio and Via Segesta, on the way to the cemetery. But, at the intersection of Via Alessandro Volta and Viale Leonardo da Vinci, the drivers didn't give a rat's ass about the pedestrians trying to cross. That morning, on my side of the curb, an older woman was trying to cross. I took her arm, put my hand up for the traffic to stop, and we crossed safely, amid honking horns. We were both headed to the cemetery. She introduced herself as Signora Bomano and asked about me. She chuckled when I said I was born in New York City, as her sister and aunt live in Brooklyn. She said she had visited many times but that her husband, who's passed away, had wanted to stay in Sicily. She said it was bruta (brutal) being alone. As we approached the cemetery, we both purchased flowers and went our separate ways.

As I entered the main gate, I decided to stop at the office and inquire about my two great-uncles who died of influenza and cholera in the early 1900's. I sat with the clerk as he checked the Ossuary Registry books – and found them! He said he would show me where they were buried in Section 2, Ossuary #2. I couldn't believe it. We walked through the cemetery to the mass grave where I placed flowers.

I photographed other gravestones, visited the three Lorenzo Milanos and Mama Sanfilippo's graves, then I stopped at the office again to ask about my elusive great-grandfather, Giuseppe Maria Vivona. The manager searched the registry books for a five-year span, but there was no listing. I decided that on another day, I would ask if I could sit and peruse the books for the time span of 1900 through 1925.

Walking back along Corso Garibaldi, there were tons of motorcycles in the streets. It must have been that time of year; as two years ago, the church on the other side of town, had held the blessing of the helmets. I asked my friend Enzo about this custom. He said it is only a local tradition, less than twenty years old, that takes place during the festival of Saint Rita of Cascia from May 20th through May 22nd. The year after the death of a young motorcyclist mechanic who died from drugs, the motorcyclists of Castellammare del Golfo and neighboring areas, decided to form a club to remember him with the blessing of the helmets.

I had a delicious late dinner at Trattoria La Maidda: a regular salad with tomato, carrots and eggplant, ravioli stuffed with grouper and topped with pistachio sauce and four prawns, with heads and all. It was an adventure extracting the prawns. As I sat outside, I heard French, German, English and Italian being spoken along with many accents (American, British, Australian). The tourists had begun to descend upon the town.

After dinner, it was time for another passeggiata, gelato and more landscape photography.

FRIDAY, MAY 11, 2018

When I opened the balcony shutters the next morning, it promised to be another beautiful day. Felice and I had caffé normale at the Tipicamente Bar. We spoke about many things including my visit to Professore Tinnirello. He also told me that Elena's grandfather, Nicolo Como, whom I met two years earlier, had passed away in September of 2016. I was sad to hear the news. Meanwhile, everyone stopped by to say ciao. I told Felice he should run for sindaco (mayor). He laughed.

It was time to go to the cemetery where I took photographs for about three hours, along with paying respects to family members. It was weird but I felt very much at home there.

After leaving the cemetery, I walked along the other side of Via Segesta and saw a crowd of people outside Pasticceria 2000. I looked in the window and saw miniature pastries. My mouth watered, so I went in, perused the display cases, and saw the little rum babas, my favorite. I ordered one and it was served on a mini-dish with a mini-fork. It was soaked and dripping with rum. OMG! Delicious.

I walked to Villa Comunale and decided to WhatsApp my husband, Vito, as it was after 10:00 a.m. his time. The reception was good there, as it was diagonally across the street from the Comune offices. We had a good conversation and got caught up on all the news.

After the phone call, I took a walk around and found myself at Café Garibaldi for a gelato. I had a great conversation with Elisabetta who told me Vito would open their second shop, I Mille, that very week. It would offer sandwiches and arancini (fried rice balls filled with peas, meat, cheese, and sauce). The new shop was a little further down the Corso, towards the new hotel where Leo worked.

On my way back to the B&B, I stopped at the salumeria (delicatessen) Gastronomia L'Angelo Del Boungustaio for a sandwich and water. As Signor Vito Fontana took my order, he saw me looking and smiling at the cartolinas on the wall. He laughed and yelled to his wife, "Vero Beach is here." Too funny.

Staircase on the left of Villa Comunale

SATURDAY, MAY 12, 2018

Another lovely morning.

I almost didn't recognize Café Garibaldi as Vito Alfano had painted his tables, added tablecloths and replaced his chairs with white ones. It looked very nice.

As I ordered my cappuccino and a pistachio cornetto, I heard my name being called by Enzo and Leonardo. They were out for an early morning walk. Enzo ordered but Leonardo continued on his walk. That morning we talked about many things including the upcoming tourist season and Enzo and Santina's hiatus to their summer home in

Alcamo. His two sons were coming from Germany and Bologna to spend twenty days in the countryside.

Enzo offered to drive me to the cemetery. I said it wasn't necessary but he said, "Andiamo." He said today was the open market and the area would be jammed packed with people. As always, he was correct. He dropped me off at the gate and we said, "Ciao."

Wooo-Hooo!

The office was open. As I walked in, the manager and I both said, "Buongiorno." I showed him my pre-written notes asking if I could look at the exhumation registers for the years 1900 through 1920. In addition, I showed the manager my family history charts and the letter I received from the Mayor's office about photographing gravestones.

He said, "You are a Milano?"

"Yes."

"Many Galatioto's and Milano's married. Andiamo."

He took me to see the small Galatioto mausoleum along the walkway. It was open, but in disrepair with an "Avvisio" sign on the door. I'd seen that on a prior day and took some photos of the graves inside. I asked if there was anything I could do to stop exhumations, but he said it was not possible. It made me very sad.

We went back to the office, and I was given the Ossuary Registry books, which took two hours to look through. I found NOTHING for my great-grandfather Giuseppe Maria Vivona.

Where the hell is he?

I continued walking through the cemetery taking photographs and found the Como mausoleum where Signor Nicolo Como had been laid to rest and paid my respects. Along the way, I helped an eighty-five-year-old woman who was climbing the ladder with no one nearby. She handed me the dead flowers and the vases. I threw out the flowers and filled the vases with water for her. She couldn't thank me enough. It was amazing to see how many older people climbed up and down those ladders every day hauling water, flowers, candles, etc.

Mid-afternoon, I walked back to the Villa Comunale as it was the best place for a Wi-Fi connection. I wanted to call Vito back in the States. WhatsApp was a little tricky but we were able to have a decent conversation with many beeps and drops but it worked and was free.

Shortly after the call, I heard someone speak English. I looked at the couple and said, "UK, US, or...?" They laughed as introductions were made. They were Deirdre and Roger from the UK. They had lived in Australia, China and the USA. We talked about many things: Brexit, Trump, education, haves/have nots, etc. It was a great conversation. He mentioned that he did ceramics (rogerlawceramics.com) and was a founding creator of the British satirical show "Spitting Image." They were very nice and interesting people. When they asked why I was there, I gave them the short version. They couldn't get over how my grandparents had lived in the town. They travel the world and liked Sicily so much they were staying in Castellammare del Golfo for another eight days. I figured we'd see each other around and was looking forward to more heated discussions.

I then meandered to Trattoria La Maidda for a lunch of risotto with veggies and a small green salad with aqua frizzante.

Heavenly!

SUNDAY, MAY 13, 2018

It was a beautiful Sunday and the streets were packed with people for the morning passeggiata (stroll). It was the time to see (and be seen by) everyone and chat along the way. Many tourists were among the crowd.

How could I tell?

The conservative dress code had obviously changed, as shorts, tees, jeans, flip-flops and sneakers of every shape and color were everywhere. And I had been afraid to bring my Easy Spirit sneakers, explorer shoes, Gloria Vanderbilt jeans and capris. At least my excuse was the trek to the cemetery to take photos.

As I walked to the Corso Garibaldi for breakfast and then up to the Villa Comunale, people stopped me to say, "Buongiorno," as we had seen each other in passing many times.

When I reached the Villa, the view stunned me. (Yes, I know it's the same photo but it's a fantastic view that's etched in my brain.)

I stood at the far railing and soaked it all in. As I turned around, I saw Roger and Deirdre again. We had a long chat and I discovered that when Roger lived in Australia he worked with the aborigines on their land. He told of the different rules and norms between the aborigines and whites. For example, men who didn't spear hunt helped the women. It was an eye-opener to say the least. They were there until Saturday, so I figured I might run into them again.

Note: There were videos on YouTube about Roger Law. He was quite a character. He reminded me of my British friend Freddy St. John-Lloyd.

I stopped in at the Chiesa Madrice. Services were at 11:00 a.m. and 6:00 p.m., but I was able to take a couple of photos. Then it was down all the stairs to the marina.

I walked La Passeggiata, while the fishermen sold their catches with kids darting here and there. I looked at the Penelope Tour Boat poster. It traveled the coastline but I wanted to find out if it had routes other than San Vito Lo Capo, Scopello and Zingaro. I had been to those places already.

After climbing back up the stairs, I meandered and found a small artists' shop, Harafi. It was open, so I went in, perused, and bought a few things, including handmade olive oil soaps. I enjoyed strolling around town and browsing.

It's funny but before I left the States, my friends asked me if I was afraid to travel alone. I said, "No. I know the town, the people and feel safe. Plus, I enjoy soaking up the atmosphere by myself." Two years ago, my cousin Bernardo graciously escorted me around the entire time. That was wonderful, but being on my own did add an extra layer of mystery and excitement. Maybe it was the explorer in me rising to the challenge. Anyway, I enjoyed it.

It was around 3:00 p.m. and I decided to have a late lunch. God knows how many restaurants I'd passed during my daily strolls around town, including a few in Piazza Europa. On the recommendation of a young man who'd commented on my Facebook posting, I decided to try Il Gitano Ristorante All'antica. I ordered spiral pasta with tomatoes, garlic, and almond pesto, a side order of grilled veggies (mushroom, eggplant, and two kinds of zucchini), bread, and aqua frizzante. He was correct, the food was fantastic. I thanked him for the great restaurant tip.

I saw my cousin Elena while walking back to the B&B. We went for caffé normale at Tipicamente. She was always working, so it was wonderful to spend some time with her. We walked back to the B&B where many people always congregated and talked to her husband, Felice. Again, I told him that he should run for mayor. He translated for everyone and they all laughed.

When everyone was leaving, I chose to stretch my legs as far as Piazza Petrolo, which was just down Via Alberto Mario, past the fruit and veggie vendor in Piazza Europa and across the street. The view of the evening sky was so very different than during the day. In addition, the evening passeggiata was in full swing.

MONDAY, MAY 14, 2018

When I opened the balcony shutters, the morning air hit me, warm and moist. The sky was overcast. I grabbed my backpack and headed out to see Vito Alfano. Ah, a cappuccino, a prosciutto and cheese croissant, were a great way to start the day. After chatting with Vito, I started the twenty-minute, one-mile walk to the cemetery. I was really glad I'd packed my Easy Spirit slip-on sneakers.

It was very quiet at the cemetery that morning. While taking photos I passed the mausoleum for the Galatioto family, where three Milano women had been laid to rest. I was upset that an Avviso (public notice) was still on the gate.

Exhumation? Now what the hell do I do?

This may be a question for our dinner discussion with Cousin Salvatore at the end of the week. We were able to save our binonno (great-grandfather) but this may be out of our control. I left when the cemetery closed for lunch.

Walking back along Via Segesta I saw Roger and Deirdre coming out of Bar Pasticceria 2000. We said hello and they told me they'd gone to the cemetery the day before and didn't understand why they exhumed the bodies when it appeared they had "...bloody space. It is barbaric."

I was glad I saw them because the prior morning I observed them reading actual books at the Villa Comunale.

My kind of people.

So, before leaving the B&B that morning, I put two of the bookmarks I'd purchased at Corey's Pharmacy (Ocean Drive, Vero Beach, FL U.S.A.) in my pocket. Corey's supports local Vero Beach artists and sells various items. Those particular bookmarks folded over the page and closed magnetically, so they wouldn't slip out. They were also decorated with miniature pictures. They thanked me, after more chatting we said, "Ciao!"

When I passed by the B&B, Felice said he and Elena would pick me up at 3:00 p.m. to go to Lina's (Elena's mom) for caffé normale. I couldn't go empty handed, so I insisted that we stop on the way for pastries. I knew the exact shop, Bar Pasticceria 2000.

Since the Wi-Fi connection is decent on Via Sole, I Whatsapp'd my Vito. He said there was a tornado in the Acreage and one headed for Port St. Lucie. I could only hope it didn't hit Vero Beach.

After that cheerful news, I needed to clear my head. My feet just meandered and via another route, I ended up on Via Puccini where I saw my friend Leo Gallo. He was getting into a car and on his way to the airport to pick up Cristina. She was returning from Spain after visiting her father who'd had surgery. I told Leo to be safe driving and to hug Cristina for me.

Lunchtime!

Vito Alfano had just opened *I Mille,* a new lunch shop at the end of Corso Garibaldi and I stopped in.

Wow!

So many aromas just hit me in the face. After perusing the menu, I ordered an arancini, which was a rice ball filled with peas, tomatoes and meat, and sautéed in a little olive oil in a black cast iron pan. It's a Sicilian specialty. It was fantastic, as it just melted in my mouth.

It was time to get back to the B&B to freshen up. As promised, Elena and Felice picked me up and we stopped for pastries at Bar Pasticceria 2000. I purchased a large assortment of mini pastries including rum babas, cassetelle, cannoli, and cassatas. We continued on our way to Lina's where I met Elena's two-year-old nephew, Gabriele. Lina made the caffé normale in a small metal espresso pot, which brought back memories.

You know the one I'm talking about.

We visited for a while and I showed Lina the Milano family history chart. She began to see all the connections between herself, her mother Caterina and my branch of the family. Two "shots" and two pastries later, we were on our way. Elena had to work, so Lina, Gabriele, Felice, Elena, and I hopped into the car. I got to see another part of town and tried to connect the roads in my head. Elena dropped Felice and me at the B&B and then headed off with her mom and nephew.

I had a wonderful late night snack at Vernaci's, one scoop of bacio gelato (dark chocolate with huge hazelnuts).

TUESDAY, MAY 15, 2018

Before I left my room that morning, I again formulated some questions in Italian for the cemetery manager. Such as:

"What needs to be done to stop the exhumation of over a dozen bodies?"

"Is there a fee to be paid? If so, cuando?"

"Do I need to hire someone to clean and paint the casa?"

My mind would not turn off that morning.

Why?

The thought of exhuming bodies made me sick and sad.

At Café Garibaldi, Vito told me his mom made an apple cake. I nodded and said, "Si, of course if your mom baked it, I have to try it with my cappuccino." I decided to sit on the back patio and asked Vito where the opposite doorway led. He said it was to the hotel.

Hotel?

That day I had a mission at the cemetery, so seeking out the front entrance of the hotel had to wait until the following day.

Ever since I saw the "Avviso" signs all around the cemetery, they bugged me. But especially the notice on the door of the Galatioto's private mausoleum.

Why?

Because there were three Milano's buried there - Lucia, Rosaria and Vita, all married to Galatioto men. Yes, the house needed a cleaning inside and touch-up paint on the outside, but at least six of the twelve graves in it had fairly new stones. In addition, Vita's grave had fresh flowers in the attached vase.

What the hell?

As I arrived, thankfully the manager was at the front gate. I said, "Buongiorno" and handed him the paper on which I'd written my questions that morning. He knew I did not speak Italian, nor the dialect, but we did our best to communicate. The manager had been very helpful over the past two weeks, but he shook his head and said that it had already been decided.

What the hell? Is it me?

I just don't understand the practice of exhumation after so many years. As Roger, the Brit, pointed out to me the day before, "There's enough bloody room here, so why do it?" I was a little depressed after speaking with the manager, but I continued to photograph the old, faded and neglected stones, as I knew sooner or later, these people would be exhumed. I left around noon.

I needed to clear my head, so I walked to Piazza Petrolo, sat, and watched the water. Eventually I calmed down. I continued the circuit and found myself at Trattoria La Maidda, where I ordered fried calamari, Sicilian style fries, and aqua frizzante. It was another wonderful late lunch with great service by Roberto.

And I topped it off with a cup of pistachio gelato at Vernaci's.

Walking back, I was on the left-hand sidewalk, which was maybe two feet wide. I was about to pass the same man I always saw at that location. We both sidestepped in the same direction, so we ended up face-to-face.

"Sorry. Scusa," I said.

In Ital-ish (like Spanglish from the movie?), he said, "You speak English. Where are you from?"

I told him I was a native New Yorker from Florida.

He laughed, showed me his New York drivers' license, and said, "I am Giuseppe Sabella. I live in Lindenhurst and work for Whole Foods."

His brother owned the fish store in town that I passed every morning, and his sister, Josephine, ran the butcher shop across the street. He brought me over to meet her.

"I have seen you many times," I said, "even two years ago when I was here last."

Giuseppe said he came back to Castellammare del Golfo yearly to visit his father and family for three months. Sometimes he took Meridiana Airlines, which was less expensive and a direct flight to Palermo from JFK Airport, but they'd changed their operation times to just June, July, August, and possibly September.

He asked me my name, so I told him.

"Lorenzo Milano, who did construction? And his wife, Maria?"

I told him that Lorenzo, was my father's first cousin. Giuseppe couldn't believe it. And when I mentioned Lorenzo's son, Salvatore, in Pisa, they both went ballistic. They could not believe the connections. I said that my grandfather Rosario Milano was Lorenzo's zio (uncle).

Giuseppe said, "Mama Mia."

I said, "Dio Mio!"

It was an interesting day to say the least. Back at the B&B, I uploaded my photos and wrote notes so I wouldn't forget anything.

WEDNESDAY, MAY 16, 2018

Yikes!

As I stuck my head out from under the covers, I felt ice-cold air. I checked my phone and found it was 45F / 7C, and it was another day with lots to do. I dressed in my heavy jeans, socks, long sleeve shirt and windbreaker. I was so glad to have packed a few warm items. I put some laundry together and went next door to see Maria from New York City, who owns the Lavanderia Martinico laundry service. Everything would be ready after 4:00 p.m. the following day.

After a breakfast of cappuccino and a cassetelle at Tipicamente (Vito was closed), I walked up Corso Bernardo Matterelle where I saw many schoolkids going into the large assembly hall next to the Comune's main office.

As I got to the Villa Comunale there was more activity. I asked a young man what was going on, and he said there was a concert by the middle school kids at 10:30 a.m., "but it might be later." More kids with instruments made their way into the park and began practicing.

I saw Roger and Deirdre having their morning caffé normale. They waved and invited me over, so we chatted awhile. Roger was writing an article about an artist friend who was dying. He hoped to be back in England over the weekend to see her.

The concert began and I stayed for an hour then I walked to Piazza Petrolo. While perusing the restaurant sidewalk boards, advertising their meals, a woman stepped out and asked if I was English. I said I am from the States and only speak English. She laughed, introduced herself as Annmarie, and said she was born in Brooklyn but was six years old when her family moved back to Sicily. Funny, as I told her I was born in New York City. We both laughed and started a conversation about New York. She asked if I wanted to have lunch, and I said I would, but only a small pizza, as I couldn't eat a huge one. Annmarie, the owner of Ristorante Pizzeria Mistral, said she would make it a little smaller.

As the winds were blowing hard off the sea, I went inside and sat at a window with a view. After chatting some more, I ordered a pizza with cheese and grilled eggplant and aqua frizzante. They baked the pizza in a wood burning oven. How did I know this?

The wood was piled up outside in the corner.

OMG! To die for. It was delicious and had a wonderful crust.

And of course, to end the meal, I enjoyed a caffé normale, and watched the activity in the Piazza.

Earlier I had mentioned to Deirdre and Roger that the Castle had a fantastic museum. They asked me the operational times, but I didn't know. I waddled out of the restaurant and figured since I was nearby, I would check the hours for them. Better yet, I took a photo so I wouldn't forget. My feet carried me up Via Castello, Via Puccini and Corso Garibaldi.

Guess who was sitting on the bench across from Tipicamente? Deirdre and Roger!

Before I forgot, I told them about the museum hours and they thanked me. Roger told more stories about: his time in Australia in Bondi Beach, when they lived on the West End of London, traveling across the States, time spent in the Village in New York City, his art, and his family. Plus, we compared world events, years ago and current, how climate changed in their hometown, Trump, etc. I mentioned that I knew all about the Village as I had hung out with Peter Yarrow, Paul Stookey, Bob Dylan, and others. I'd listened to their music and heard the anti-war speeches.

"Unbelievable," Roger said, shaking his head.

They were two fascinating and thought-provoking people; we could talk for hours. When they left for the museum, I went back to the B&B to upload my photos and write.

THURSDAY, MAY 17, 2018

It was another chilly morning so long dark jeans, socks, a heavy tee shirt, sneakers, and my windbreaker were the outfit for the day.

At the Café, I ordered a cappuccino, a square nut pastry and pomegranate juice. I also gave Vito a few euros to pay for Enzo's coffee.

Why?

Enzo would not take a euro from me for gas to the Mothia Salt Pans nor allow me to pay for the admission. Since I paid for his coffee in advance, when he got back from his vacation in Alcamo, he couldn't argue with me.

Earlier, Vito Alfano had mentioned that the back courtyard of the Café led to a hotel on the other side. So, I explored some new streets and found the little hotel, Le Plejadi (Via Nunzio Nasi 41, 91014, Castellammare del Golfo, Sicily). Ironically, one of my great-uncles, Antonino Vivona, died at age fifteen on the same street in house number 135.

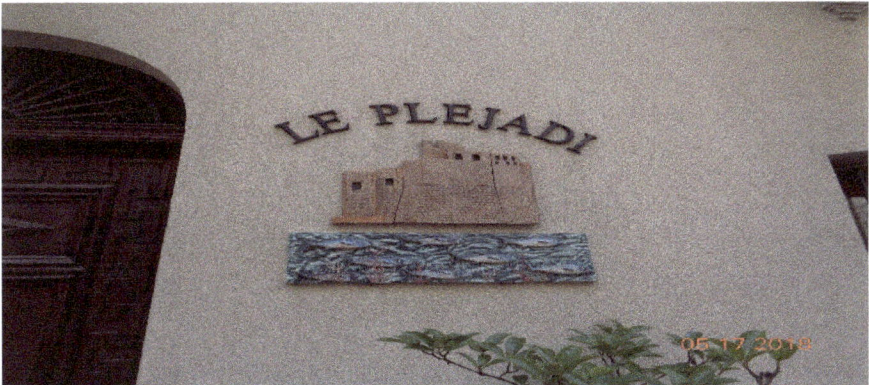

I continued walking and found another way down to Piazza Europa to the fruit and vegetable vendor where I bought more fresh strawberries.

As I was leaving, a young man, who introduced himself as Salvatore, asked if I was interested in buying fish. I told him that I was visiting and had no kitchen. We talked for a little bit and I told him my family was from town. Just then, I heard Felice call my name, so I turned and waved.

Salvatore asked, "How do you know that man?"

"Felice is my cugino."

"Ah, I also know him," Salvatore said.

We both laughed, as everyone in town knows everyone.

When I stopped by the B&B to put my strawberries away, I planned to ask Felice about the sindaco (mayor). But, when I turned the corner, there was a man speaking to Felice.

Oh my!

His was the voice I'd heard the other night that I couldn't place and it was driving me nuts. I'd met him two years earlier but couldn't remember his name. He spoke Italian and French only, no English.

I pointed to the man and said, "Felice, this is the voice I heard the other night."

Felice then introduced me to Giuseppe Bambinio, who said he recognized me.

All too funny.

Getting back to the mayor, I told Felice that I wanted to stop by the mayor's office to introduce myself and thank him for the positive response about photographing the gravestones. Felice did not think it was necessary, as the mayor's term was ending, but I said I wanted to do it. Felice said his office was on the first floor (our second floor) of the Comune building.

"Grazie. Ciao. A presto," I said.

So, I started my walk back up to the Villa Comunale, as the office was across the street. I took the elevator to the first floor and was met by a carabineri. I showed him the letter and explained that I wanted to see the mayor if possible. He brought me to the office and explained my request to two women. One woman spoke some English, read the letter, made a phone call and said, "He will be here within fifteen minutes." I thanked her and waited on the bench outside the office. I saw the mayor coming down the hall; however, two other people approached him first. After they left, I was next.

I introduced myself and showed him the letter. He smiled. I thanked him for the courtesy of the reply letter and the permission to photograph within the cemetery. We shook hands and he gave me a pen with his name, as mayor, stamped on it.

Around 2:30 p.m., I had lunch at Trattoria La Maidda. I saw Roberto, grabbed an outside table, ordered a caprese salad, and grilled vegetables with aqua fizzante. And of course, the bread and oil arrived shortly after.

What a feast. And yes, I'll include the photos.

After that lunch, I had to walk. At the Villa Comunale, I saw Deirdre and Roger who invited me to have tea with them at Tipicamente. We sat and chatted about many topics including some of the authors they'd read. I was always looking for new authors, so in addition to Peter Robb (Australian), I had Phillip Kerr to look up. Deirdre and Roger, very interesting people, were to leave on Saturday, so just in case we didn't run into each other before then, we said goodbye.

I continued down Corso Garibaldi as I wanted to stop in to see Cristina at Sikelia Sicilian Souvenirs. She returned from Spain the prior Monday. We talked about many topics, including immigration, why I don't speak the dialect nor Italian, internment camps around the world, her work in Columbia for two years, the organization Open Arms, the Palestinians, Trump, etc. She was such a smart and beautiful woman. She said to stop by as much as I want before I left.

Then it was back to the Villa Comunale, as the Wi-Fi seemed to be the best there for speaking to my Vito via WhatsApp. He was on the west coast of Florida near Bradenton, taking in the sights and visiting friends. We had a great conversation, but I wished he was with me to share it all.

FRIDAY, MAY 18, 2018

It was a lazy but exciting morning; I would finally meet my cousin Salvatore after two years of emails and texts. I took my time getting ready. As I walked the Corso, the swallows, pigeons and sea gulls flew around me, each singing their own song. It was a pleasure to hear.

I was surprised when I reached Cafe Garibaldi, as I saw Enzo and his neighbor Leonardo.

"Ciao. Buongiorno," we said.

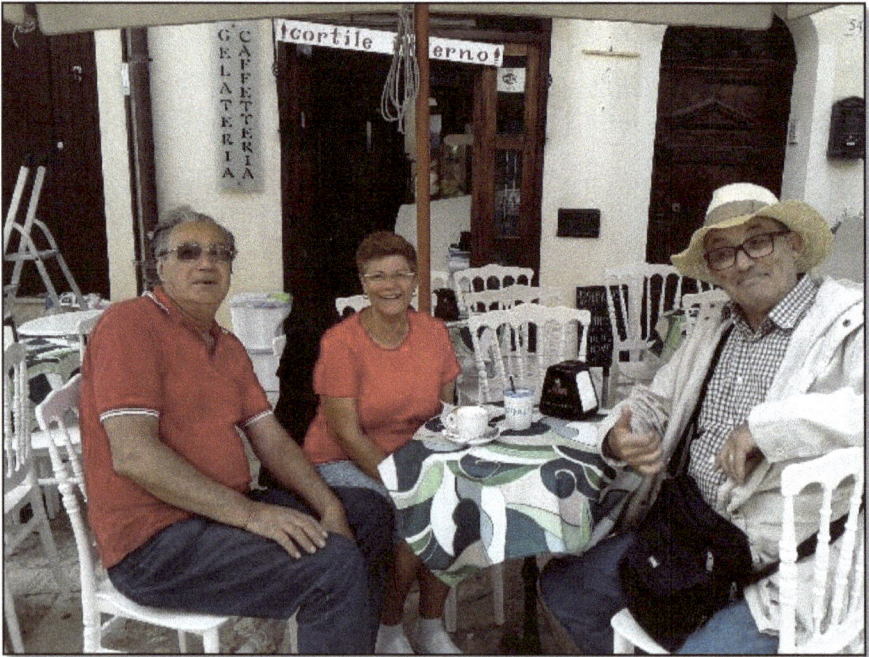

I asked Enzo if he'd had a nice time in Alcamo. He showed me his scraped hands and said how he'd worked for days getting the house ready for his two son's twenty-day visit in June.

We sat, talked with Vito, drank cappuccino, and ate cornettos. When we were done, Enzo said, "Andiamo. I want to walk to Petrolo." During our walk, we talked about all the restoration and ongoing new construction. He talked about how the Petrolo area was a manufacturing zone when he was born. There were many wine and grappa distilleries, where his father had been a master distiller.

He couldn't show me the house where he grew up as it had been destroyed to make room for progress, meaning for more updated housing. We walked the circuit back to the Garibaldi and Mattarella intersection. He continued home, and I to the Villa -- and beyond.

Later in the day, I heard from Cousin Salvatore. He and Monika had visited Maria in the morning and were then in Salemi and Partinico. He asked where we should meet.

I wrote, "Trattoria La Maidda."

He replied, "7:30 p.m."

I didn't know if reservations were needed for Friday night, so I stopped in to see Roberto and Gaspare at La Maidda. They asked how many people. When I told them, they said, "No problema."

Ok, that's done.

I was so excited as I got ready. When I left the B&B, at 7:20 p.m., I saw Felice and told him I was finally meeting Salvatore in a little while. Felice said to say, "Ciao" for him and Elena.

Along the way up, I saw Giuseppe Sabella from Long Island at his brother's fish store, stopped, and said, "Buona sera." Then I ran into the woman I'd helped in the cemetery. She introduced me to her daughter, who kept saying, "Grazie. Grazie."

"Nessun problema," I said.

When I arrived at Trattoria La Maidda, Roger and Deirdre were there! They thanked me for the restaurant recommendation, as it was a great way to wrap up their trip. Unfortunately, they had to leave on Saturday.

Roberto showed me to the table and a little while later, I saw Salvatore coming through the door. Exchanging photos online was one thing, but when physically seeing the man was quite different. I was shocked, as Salvatore looked so much like my father. I couldn't get over it.

Salvatore spoke with Roberto, who showed him to my table. I got up and we simultaneously said, "Ciao," and hugged and kissed. Monika was not with him, so I knew there must be a problem with Maria. He said they visited with Maria that morning and she looked fine and was so happy to see them. But earlier in the afternoon, the assisted living facility called and said they were bringing Maria to the hospital in Alcamo. He and Monika went there and it appeared that Maria had a temperature and an infection. Monika stayed with her while Salvatore kept his appointment with me.

I told him to go back to the hospital.

"No. I wanted to finally meet and visit with you."

So, after we ordered dinner, we exchanged stories and discovered new pieces of family information. We both enjoyed the food and company.

During dinner, Salvatore received a phone call from Monika and the way I saw his body sag, I knew it was not good news. He told me a sonogram showed a growth on Maria's pancreas. He said they did tests last week, including x-rays and a CT scan with dye, and had been told everything was okay.

"It sounds like they misdiagnosed her condition," I said.

He said he was thinking the same thing.

Salvatore told me that for Christmas, he flew Maria up to Pisa to be with him, Monika, and her two grandsons, Loris (yes, another Lorenzo) and Juri. He mentioned to his mother that maybe she could

232

stay for a little longer, but Maria was adamant. She wanted to go back home because she visited her husband, Lorenzo, daily at the cemetery. Salvatore said she needed around the clock care, which she received at Mother Teresa's, although he couldn't continue to commute between Sicily and Pisa to check on her. His older brother Renzo was unavailable to help. Salvatore explained that he made arrangements at his home, so Maria could receive the care she needs there. But he still needed to sway Maria to his way of thinking. Her health may leave her no choice.

After dinner, at my request, Gaspare took photos of us, using each of our phones.

Grazie Gaspare.

Salvatore wanted to drive me back, but I said, "No, grazie. It's right down the road and I will walk."

We hugged, kissed, and said, "Ciao."

He apologized because I did not meet Monika. I told him it was not a problem, as Maria was his priority and we will see each other again. I hoped he could reach a compromise with Maria, so she can get the care she needs under his watchful eye.

SATURDAY, MAY 19, 2018

Crap!

I woke up with a stuffy head so I took an Advil Cold and Sinus. I moseyed out onto Cafe Garibaldi where I gave Vito Alfano the crocheted towels. He thanked me and brought over my cappuccino, pistachio cornetto, and peach juice. He asked if I'd finally met Salvatore.

"Yes! We had a wonderful visit."

After breakfast, I set out for the cemetery, stopped at the flower vendor and visited binonno Lorenzo, his son Lorenzo, my two great-uncles, Cousin Lorenzo, Nicolo Como and Mama Sanfilippo. When I was at Cousin Lorenzo's mausoleum, a woman from the Randazzo family, across from him, asked where Maria was, as she had not recently seen her. I told her she was at the Mother Teresa assisted living facility. She was sad to hear it. I took photos for another two hours.

After my visit to the cemetery, and on my way to lunch, I stopped at the farmicia for cough medicine, just in case my cough got worse.

Dammit!

I had a late lunch at Annmarie's Ristorante Pizzeria Mistral. She was happy to see me and we continued our previous conversation about New York City and our families. On her recommendation, I ordered the polpo al agriglia (grilled octopus) and aqua frizzante. Annmarie asked about a salad, but I said it would be too much food.

"No problem, I will add more greens onto the plate for you."

OMG! Too die for.

The octopus was a large portion with a nice salad of greens and funghi (mushrooms). I took my time, savoring all the flavors. Annmarie stopped by occasionally to check on me. She mentioned that she made fresh tiramisu.

"You're killing me," I said. "I can only eat a small portion."

She laughed and said she'd cut it small, which she did. It was so light and creamy and melted in my mouth.

Anna Maria asked where I was staying and when was I leaving. When I mentioned B&B Nonna Giò, she was surprised. She explained that her brother-in-law was Felice's godfather. We both laughed.

See, as I said before, everyone knew everyone.

SUNDAY, MAY 20, 2018

Yawoozier.

Sono stanca (I am tired), so I moved in slow motion. Funny thing that morning; when I opened the balcony door to put the bathmat out on the railing to dry, I saw a nun walking down the street – in her habit. I haven't seen that in a very long time. I tried to reach my camera in time to take a photo, but only caught a little of her.

When I walked up to the Corso, I took note of the quiet morning. It was too early for the passaggiata, but the men were already out claiming their benches.

When I saw Vito at the café, I said, "Ciao. Come va?"

He answered me in English. "I am well. But you..."

He pointed to my throat as I sounded like a frog. I told him I was allergic to everything – pollen, dust, etc. He asked if I went to the farmacia. I said I did and was given Winn Tuss (cough syrup expectorant). He gave me a thumbs-up.

I ordered cappuccino, juice (which Vito selected) and a scrumptious ham and cheese cornetto.

As soon as it arrived at the table, so did Enzo and Leonardo. They also ordered caffé normale. Enzo ordered his usual; a small ricotta filled cornetto.

We always had nice conversations with the aid of our translators. But as time rolled on, I used it less and less as I started to actually understand some of the dialect. When either Enzo or I could not think of a word, we would mime or speak into the phone. Leonardo was surprised to learn that his friend Enzo, knew English.

We always laughed with other people as they walked by and chimed in. Enzo mentioned that he'd been a city commissioner and a police officer, so they all knew him. He was quite a character.

His wife Santina was taking courses online, so she was wrapped up with school. I told Enzo that the nuns at university called me "a lifer" as I only took one course a semester, because I worked, commuted and was on the condominium board of directors. I was fifty-two years old when I finally received my Masters' Degree in Organizational Management. Enzo was complaining, as he now had to fend for himself – making caffé normale, his lunch, etc. I told him that for many years, Santina catered to him and now it was her turn.

No sympathy for him!

He burst out laughing and said, "Dio mio."

Leonardo just shook his head and left for his walk.

Enzo and I walked down towards the marina, where I took videos and photos. I never got tired watching all the activity. After a long stroll, we walked back up to the Villa Comunale, where we talked with everyone who was around and then parted saying, "See you tomorrow."

On Facebook, I'm friends with some people in town, from whom I have asked genealogy and family history questions. Ironically, I heard from one man, Matteo Vivona, who sent me a Messenger text. I viewed the photos of beautiful handmade items and asked if the store, Io e La My Sicilian Bag, was in Castellammare del Golfo.

"Yes."

So, on my way back to the B&B, I stopped in, introduced myself to Matteo and his beautiful wife, who was the artist. He was stunned to see me.

Back at my room, another funny thing happened. I was on the balcony, reading and minding my own business, when I saw a man and his wife dressed "to the nine's," open a garage door and drive out in a white Mercedes. They were gone awhile. In the meantime, a blue car came, parked in front of the garage and the gentleman left the car blinkers on. A short while later, the Mercedes came back and continually honked his horn.

Uh oh.

The wife and a teenager stepped out of the car with suitcases. Mr. Mercedes parked the car and walked right under my balcony. I explained that I don't speak Italian, but I communicated with hand motions that the people from the car walked up the street and turned left. He thanked me. Shortly thereafter, the owners of the blue car returned and drove away. About a half an hour later, Mr. Mercedes pulled his car into the garage.

Comical, but that's what happens here. Mr. Mercedes assumed that I knew what had happened.

Why?

Most days the neighborhood ladies were either on the sidewalk or had their balcony doors open and saw everything that went on outside. As a matter of fact, around the corner of Via Sole #2, there were two nice ladies who always saw me in the morning and said, "Bourgiorno." They were always observing when they were home.

I heard from Salvatore much later that day. His mom, my cousin Maria, was still in the hospital in Alcamo. He and Monika were packing as they had to fly back to Pisa but he wanted to stop by. I said that he needed to be calm, take care of himself, finish his packing and go to the airport. I told him we would meet again and was happy we'd had dinner together the other night.

I was too beat to even eat dinner, although I did have my banana and strawberries.

It's an early night for me.

MONDAY, MAY 21, 2018

I woke up feeling much better. I still had the cough but my head and ear congestion were just about gone, although my nose was still running.

 Lots of people were out that morning, including Giuseppe Sabella from Long Island to whom I said, "Buongiorno."

He laughed. "Good morning, New York."

He's another character. Speaking of characters, after I ordered my cappucino, mandarin juice and an apple tart at Vito's, Enzo and Leonardo came strolling by. More caffé normale, water and cornettos were ordered.

Enzo was all discombobulated that morning. I asked what had happened.

"Microsoft," he said. "It took over the computer. Santina was upset as she was writing her thesis and it took hours to get it back."

I shook my head. "You should've texted me, as I knew all too well. Windows hijacked our laptop for over eight hours. Once it stopped, I had Microsoft re-install the older version of Windows. It was a big-time mess."

So, again, technology was the topic of conversation. Funny because that was what brought Enzo and I together over two years earlier.

That morning, we had an audience, as lots of people stopped by to add their two cents into the conversation. After breakfast, I headed to Piazza Petrolo for more olives and strawberries to replenish my nosh stash. I went back to the B&B to put them in the fridge and then visited Cristina at Sikelia Sicilian Souvenirs.

She was happy to see me and invited me to sit down and talk. I gave her two small gifts which she thanked me for. I mentioned this before but to refresh your memory, Cristina is from Catalonia Spain, so we discussed all that was happening there. Plus, the work she did in Colombia and elsewhere around the world. She's a very interesting woman. As we talked, people came in and out of the store. While she was helping some folks from Germany, a woman tried to get my attention. I explained I was just visiting but I showed her a few things. When she started asking questions, I said, "I'll get the chief." She laughed, as she understood what I'd said. Eventually Cristina was able to help her. I stayed for about two hours and said that I would stop in again tomorrow, as I was leaving Wednesday.

She said, "No, not already? The time goes by so fast."

Exactly my sentiments.

Time for lunch!

Since I hadn't eaten anything after breakfast yesterday, I decided to go see Annmarie at the Ristorante Pizzeria Mistral. I ordered a large salad with arugula, greens, mushrooms, shaved parmesan cheese, tuna, tomatoes and buffalo mozzarella, along with aqua frizzante. The salad was fantastic. Annmarie also gave me a little scoop of the lemon granita for dessert. She knew I didn't like to waste food and went out of her way to make small portions for me. She was a very sweet lady. I met her husband, the restaurant's pizza maker, and her two children when they stopped by after school.

Back to the B&B to freshen up and relax before going to the Feast of Saint Rita (saint of the impossible). It began on Saturday and ran for three days. That day it did not start until 8:00 p.m., but I wanted to walk up while it was still light out, as I was unsure about the exact location. I walked my route to the cemetery and, as I reached the top of Via Segesta, I saw all the yellow tape. As I skirted around the roadblock, kids were enjoying rides and there were miles of vendor tables with all kinds of clothes, ceramics, food, etc. It reminded me of a New York street fair. After walking around for a couple of hours, I left. The thought of having to pack drew me back to the B&B where Felice was holding court with a group of his friends.

TUESDAY, MAY 22, 2018

Dammit!

I woke up with a stuffy head, again, but when I flung open the balcony doors, it was a beautiful sunny morning. As I walked to the Cafe, I was surprised to see Enzo already there talking with Vito. We ordered breakfast, cappuccino, juice and a ham cornetto. Google translate was very active that morning. Also, Enzo talked to Cortona.

Really?

Enzo asked about my congestion and said I should go back to the farmacia, before it got worse.

"Yes" I said, "I planned to do so."

After breakfast, we walked a little along the Corso then up to Villa Comunale to soak in the view. Then onto the farmicia, as Enzo had a prescription to pick up. As always, he was joking with everyone in the store. They all knew him. He told me, not only was he a city commissioner, building inspector and a police officer, he was also a foot patrolman with a gun. I imagined that over many years, he had been a force to be reckoned with.

When it was my turn, I told the young pharmacist behind the counter about my congestion problem and that I needed to be able to transport the medicine on the plane. He brought out a few boxes with upper respiratory pictures on them.

I turned to Enzo and asked, "Which would be better?"

The young man was surprised that I asked Enzo his opinion, so Enzo explained that I was a friend from America. So now the pharmacist couldn't do enough to help me.

Outside I teased Enzo about running for mayor. He laughed and said that many people and their families remember his job in the town.

I just wiggled my eyebrows.

We hugged, kissed, and said, "Ciao. A presto."

He was such a fantastic man. I knew I would miss sharing breakfast and walks with him.

I continued back to the B&B to drop off the meds and see Felice. He helped me check-in online with Alitalia. After I settled my bill, we chatted about my visit and my plans to return.

Afterwards, I walked down to Petrolo where I tried to memorize the view in my head, took photos, and stopped to say goodbye to Annmarie at the Ristorante Pizzeria Mistral. We had caffé normale and spoke awhile. She also told me about her B&B, gave me a card, and then I was off. I took the long way back and passed the Castle, and the juice vender with a Sicilian Cart.

I continued on and had a wonderful late lunch at Trattoria La Maidda of ravioli filled with veal and saturated in a pistachio cream sauce.

Absolutely scrumptious!

I thanked both Roberto and Gaspare for the great food and service, and then we all said, "A presto!"

I couldn't leave town without stopping by to see Vito and Elisabetta Alfano. After one more caffé normale, we said, "A presto!"

It was almost 6:00 p.m. when I arrived at Sikelia Sicilian Souvenirs. Cristina was busy with a customer, so I sat in "my chair" next to the counter. We talked about so many subjects. Before I left, she presented me with a gorgeous blue scarf. Cristina noticed that I wore many shades of blue, so it would complement my outfits.

I thanked her. We hugged, kissed, and said, "A presto!" I was sad to leave her as we had so much in common and could talk all day.

The weather turned dreary with drizzling rain, so I walked back to the B&B to write and pack. It was an early night, as I had to be up at 3:30 a.m. to be ready for my 5:00 a.m. ride to the airport.

Felice drove me to the airport. We talked about many things but the main topics were Cousin Maria, what I had accomplished and when I would return to finish the cemetery photographs. Soon we hugged, kissed, "A presto."

We parted; he to his car and me to Alitalia check-in.

What a wonderful trip!!!

BACK IN THE USA

After my return, I worked on cropping and uploading the cemetery photographs to the Find-A-Grave website. http://bit.ly/2CEH7OX

At the time of this writing, other people have added names to the site but no photos. The next time I go to Castellammare del Golfo, I will bring the list of names with me to see if the gravestones are available. If not, it will be time again to browse the Ossuary Registry books!

A presto!

Acknowledgements

As most of you know, a book is not written by only one person. It takes a worldwide village for it to come to being.

First, I want to thank my wonderful husband, Vito, for all his love and support.

Thank you to all family, friends, and strangers who tolerated and answered all my incessant questions.

Also, a big "Thank you" to the many people in The Writers Window Pane critique group at the Indian River County Main Library in Vero Beach, FL for their constructive criticism, editing and suggestions. Special thanks to Laurance H. Davis (formatting a manuscript and other tidbits), Judith Konitzer, Helen Barnet (for the maps), Dorothy Rosenfeldt, T.H. Pine, and Janet Sierzant.

Molte grazie a tutti!

About the Author

Celia A. Milano was born in New York City and raised in Westchester County New York. She has several degrees, including a Master's of Science in Management from College of St. Elizabeth, Morristown, NJ. For over 30 years, she worked as a computer software engineer in the military and petroleum industries. Retired and living in Florida she devotes her time to researching her family tree and continues to gather information to add to her book "So, Where Do I Really Come From? A Sicilian Family Tree". In her free time, she helps guide people in writing their memoirs. Celia is also on the board of directors for The Sicilian Project, a non-profit organization that offers free English instructional camps to the children in Sicily. The Sicilian Project is important to her because as a child, she was not allowed to learn the Sicilian dialect, as the thought at that time was to be "Americanized." The idea that Sicilian children will become bi-lingual and have a greater advantage in the world is very rewarding to her.